DOLOMITES

easy alpine walks

FRANZ HAULEITNER

D0300738

SUNFLOWER
BOOKS

First published 1988 by Sunflower Books
12 Kendrick Mews, London SW7 3HG, UK

PUBLISHER'S NOTE ————————————————

Unlike most of the books we publish, we have not
written, mapped out, or checked the walks in this book.
It is a translation of a volume in the first series of *walking*
books published by Bergverlag Rudolf Rother, one of
Germany's foremost publishers of mountaineering books
and periodicals. While we cannot accept responsibility
for the accuracy of the text and maps, we would be
grateful to receive your comments, which we could pass
on to the original publishers.
We rely on walkers to take along a good supply of
common sense — as well as our guides — when they go
hiking. If a route is not as described in the text and
your way ahead is not secure, return to the point of
departure. **Do not attempt to complete a walk under
hazardous conditions.** Please read the Foreword on page
5 and the General introduction on pages 6–9. Walk
safely and respect the mountains!

Translation by the staff of Sunflower Books
Photographs by the author
Walking maps by Gertrude and Wilhelm Wagner
Overview map by Pat Underwood
Printed and bound in the UK by W S Cowell Ltd, Ipswich
E/DH

CONTENTS

EASTERN DOLOMITES

Many visitors to the Dolomites would enjoy walking in the region, but they want a relaxing holiday. They are not mountaineers and would appreciate some guidance on the best short walks in the area. I believe that this is the first such book.

The Dolomites offer a wealth of rambling opportunities for the modest walker. At sub-alpine level — between the individual massifs — there are enchantingly beautiful meadowlands and larch tree forests to be explored during easy excursions 'between the mountains'. The forty-three walks in this book offer just a taste from the rich cornucopia of possibilities. You can walk to wild ravines, picturesque valleys, lonely mountain lakes, isolated huts and shelters, superb viewpoints and easily-climbed peaks. Moreover, since many of the routes are accessible by chair lift or funicular, you can often indulge in the pleasurable pursuit of 'downhill mountain-climbing'!

All of the walks in this book are fairly easy and follow well-marked routes. They are suitable for fit people of all ages, from children to the elderly. The average walking time to cover the entire route is between two and three hours; the average climb to be mastered at any one stretch is 300m/985ft. Overnight stays in shelters or guesthouses are suggested for each walk, but in no case is an overnight stay obligatory: all the walks make comfortable half-day or full-day excursions.

The presentation of each walk follows the same pattern: the ramble is described on two facing pages and illustrated with a photograph and a map. Planning information is given at the start of each walk.

I hope that everyone who uses this guide will spend many joyful hours exploring the unforgettable Dolomites.

—FRANZ HAULEITNER

Using the book
The Contents show you the plan of the book and, together with the map on pages 8–9, give you an overview of the walks. Important information is given at the start of each walk, in 'shorthand' form. A brief description of the route follows; this is illustrated on an accompanying map. A photograph is also included for each excursion — to inspire you in advance!

Grading of the walks
All of the walks in this book are easily tackled by fit people and can be done without any special training. Walking boots are not necessary; stout shoes will suffice. Note, however, that a few of the walks demand surefootedness and a head for heights. At the start of each walk the total climb (or descent) is given, *in italic type*.

Waymarking
Almost all of the walks are very well waymarked, and the route numbers are always referred to in the text.

Dangers
Although all of the walks follow country roads, tracks or well-made footpaths, remember that there is *always* a possibility of danger in the mountains — due to storm damage, rockfalls, sudden thunder- or hailstorms, etc. There are also poisonous snakes in some areas.

Walking times
The walking times given at the start of each walk are generous, but they *do not include any stops.*

Best time of year
The months suggested take into account various factors, such as when the ground is free of snow, when the funiculars operate, when the shelters are open, and when the landscape is most lovely.

Clothing and provisions

Be sure to wear stout shoes with good grip. Knee-length socks are advisable. Carry a cardigan, an anorak and some raingear as well. A small rucksack will hold these, as well as some provisions like fruit and chocolate, if you are not packing a lunch. A water flask is mandatory, and it's always a good idea to carry a whistle. You do not need to take any climbing equipment.

Glossary

In order to keep the price of this book as low as possible, the walking maps have been reproduced directly from the original German guide. Most of the information on the maps is self-explanatory and is given in the language used on local signposts (where German and Italian are both in common usage). The glossary below covers all the terms you will find on the maps or in the text. Heights are shown in metres (1 metre = 3.28 feet), but *total climb/descent* is given in feet as well.

German	English	Italian	English
Alm	pastureland	Bàita	bar, shelter
außer	outer	Bivacco (Biv.)	bivouac
Bach	stream	Capanna (Cap.)	hut, shelter
Berg	mountain	Casera (Cas.)	mountain hut
ehem.	formerly	Cima (C.)	summit, peak
Fels	rock	Col	hill
Gasthof (Ghf.)	guesthouse	Cresta	ridge
Gipfel	peak	Croda	cliff, wall
Hütte (Htt.)	hut, shelter	Forcella (Forc.)	saddle
Höhenweg/route	high-level route	Funivia	funicular, lift
ins	to, into	Lago (L.)	lake
Joch	saddle	Malga	mountain hut
Kapelle	chapel	Monte (M.)	mount
Kirche	church	Passo (Pso.)	pass
klein (Kl./kl.)	little	Pian/o	plateau
nach	to	Ponte (Pte.)	bridge
ober	upper	Pra	meadow
Paß	pass	Rifugio (Rif.)	shelter
Sattel	saddle	Rio, Rivo (R.)	river
Scharte	gap, small pass	Sass, Sasso	rock
See	lake, reservoir	Sella	saddle
Seilbahn	funicular	Sentiero	footpath
Sesselbahn	chair lift	Torre(i)	tower(s)
Spitz	peak	Torrente (T.)	stream
Tal	valley	Val, Valle (V.)	valley
verf.	ruined	Via	trail, path
Wald	forest		
Weg	path, trail		
Wssf.	waterfall		
zum	to, towards		

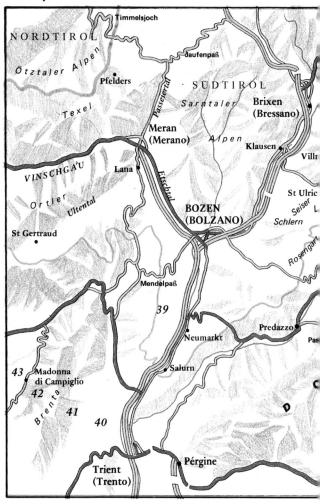

Maps

The map above shows the general location of all the walks in this book.* Each walk is illustrated with a large-scale map, so you need not purchase any special walking maps. However, a good touring map (suggested scale about 1:200,000) is essential for getting to the starting point of any walks located off the main roads shown here.

*A companion volume, *Waymarks South Tyrol*, includes many more walks in the western Dolomites and around Meran.

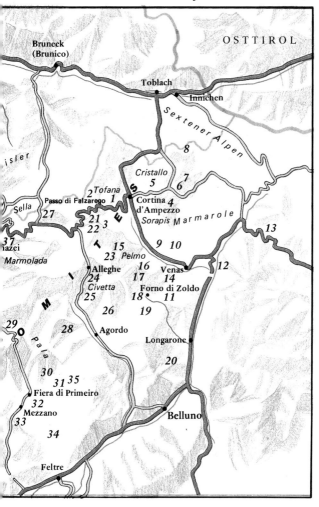

Shelters, guesthouses, restaurants
Refreshments are available at all of the shelters
described in the heading 'Overnight suggestions'.

Funiculars and lifts
Several walks in this book start from a point
reached by funicular, cabin lift or chair lift.
*Do note that many of these are only open in
July, August and September.* At other times, the
starting point may only be accessible on foot!

Approach: Cortina d'Ampezzo (1211m/3970ft), a very popular tourist centre in the upper Boite Valley

Starting point/parking: Cortina

Overnight suggestion: none, but you can get refreshments and hire boats at the lakeside restaurant

Walking time: Cortina to the lake about 1h30min; Lake Ghedina to Cadin di Sopra and back to Cortina about 1h30min; *total time under 3h*

Grade: an easy climb on good tracks and narrow mountain roads

Highest point: the Sella Belvedere (about 1485m/4870ft), reached after a *climb of 246m/805ft*

Best season: possible all year round, but at its loveliest in late autumn

---

A visit to little Lake Ghedina is one of the most popular excursions from the tourist centre of Cortina. Well-marked tracks and narrow mountain roads take you to the tranquil lake, set in a magnificent forest of conifers on the eastern slopes of Tofana. The return route continues in 'tiers' through the hamlets of Cadin di Sopra, Cadin di Sotto and Cadelverzo. In high summer this walk won't be at its best; choose instead a pristine day in late October, when the autumn colours are at their finest. The splendid

Cortina against the backdrop of Sorapis and Antelao

outlook towards the massif of the Ampezzan Dolomites in the north and northeast — especially Pomagagnon, Cristallo, Sorapis and Antelao — is never to be forgotten.

From Cortina to Lake Ghedina via the Sella Belvedere □

From Cortina take the Falzarego Pass road, heading left and climbing to the large bend to the left near the group of houses at Ronco. Turn right here, to the Villa Ideale, then half-left to the Villa Clemente (where there is a signpost). Now you're in the forest, and you will cross the bob-sleigh run on a bridge. Keep up on Route 413 and come to the crossing of the asphalt road (Route 414); here turn right (north) and climb up past the Sella Belvedere. From this lookout point on the saddle, the route — mostly level walking — skirts the eastern flanks of Tofana to reach the picturesque lake.

Return walk to Cortina via Cadin □

Follow the road heading north and curve downhill below the Sass Peron to a bridge, the Ponte de ra Sia. Don't cross the Boite; instead turn right and follow the track (Routes 408/417, later Route 415) south, gently climbing up to the hamlet of Cadin di Sopra ('Upper' Cadin), before descending again to 'Lower' Cadin and Cadelverzo. When you come to Ronco, you will again follow the Falzarego Pass road back into Cortina.

Approach: Cortina d'Ampezzo (1211m/3970ft), a popular international tourist centre in the upper Boite Valley

Parking/funicular: Falzarego Pass (2105m), accessible by car or by bus from Cortina (16km) or Andraz (6km). From the pass, take the cabin lift to the summit of Kleiner Lagazuoi.

Starting point: upper end of the cabin lift (summit of Kleiner Lagazuoi, 2750m)

Overnight suggestion: Lagazuoi Shelter (2752m, private, open from mid-June until 10 October, 14 beds, 22 bunks)

Walking time: from the top of the cabin lift to the summit 10min; from the summit back to the Falzarego Pass about 1h–1h30min; *total time 1h15min–1h45min*

Grade: an easy 'downhill mountain walk' on well-signposted paths

Highest point: Kleiner Lagazuoi (2778m/9110ft), from where there is a *descent of 673m/2205ft*

Best time of year: beginning of June until the end of October

---

Pierced and split in places by bombardments in the First World War, and later gouged open to accommodate a cabin lift and a very comfortable shelter to cater for mass tourism, Kleiner Lagazuoi is one of those Dolomite peaks where even the most casual tourist cannot but be awestruck by the nature of the mountain world. Fortunately, none of the attacks on its flanks have detracted from Lagazuoi's beauty or

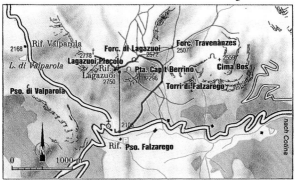

its justifiable reputation as one of the very best viewing points in the Dolomites. The walk described here affords simply splendid panoramas towards the rocky massifs of the Nuvolau Group and Croda da Lago on the southern side of the Great Dolomite Road.

From the upper end of the cabin lift to the summit of Kleiner Lagazuoi □

Pass by the shelter and follow the good footpath northwest to the summit — it's just a slight ascent.

Descent from the summit to the Falzarego Pass □

Return to the shelter and from there follow Route 402 which curves down the north side of the mountain. You'll come to a signposted fork: keep right and continue down to the Lagazuoi Saddle (2572m). From here follow Route 20 down towards the right, through a steep scree and to a narrowing of the route. Later, under the southern walls of the mountain, bear right diagonally (southwest) towards the pass.

Opposite: the Lagazuoi Shelter and behind it, in the distance, Croda da Lago. Between the two is the deep divide where the Great Dolomite Road cuts through the Falzarego Pass.

Approach: Cortina d'Ampezzo (1211m/3970ft), a very popular tourist centre in the upper Boite Valley

Starting point/parking: Ponte di Rocurto (1708m), a bridge 11km from Cortina on the Giau Pass road. Accessible by car from Cortina (via Pocol)

Overnight suggestion: Palmieri Shelter (2046m, run by the Cortina branch of the Italian Alpine Club, open from 6 June until the end of September, 10 beds, 24 bunks)

Walking time: from the Ponte di Rocurto to the lake about 1h45min–2h; return about 1h15min–1h30min; *total time under 3h30min*

Grade: an easy walk on well-signposted tracks and paths

Highest point: Palmieri Shelter (2046m/6710ft), reached after a *climb of 338m/1110ft*

Best time of year: mid-June until the end of October

Lake Federa, set on a picturesque 'terrace' above the Cortina basin, boasts an especially charming landscape. The views from here are simply superb. Of special interest, however, is the contrast between the mighty rock walls of Croda da Lago and the more distant slopes of Cristallo, Sorapis and Antelao on the other side of the Boite Valley. As soon as you set out from the Giau Pass road through a lovely mountain forest, the towers and pinnacles of the Croda da Lago Group are in sight. Then the walk around the lake itself — through lovely stands of larch and stone-pines — is an ideal opportunity for nature lovers and photographers to indulge their

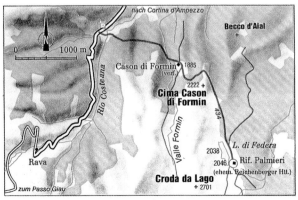

The Becco di Mezzodi rising behind Lake Federa

hobbies. The Palmieri Shelter on the banks of the lake provides a welcome overnight stopping-point, in case you idle the day away. . . .

From the Rocurto Bridge (Giau Pass road) to Lake Federa □

Follow the signposted path (Route 437) east: a few steep curves take you down to the Costeana River, which is crossed. From here it's a gentle climb up through conifers to a steep stone stair-way. At the top, turn right through the grassy Formin Valley, sparsely wooded in spruce. From here there are especially fine views towards the towers of the Croda da Lago Group. Continuing east through a light wood of larch, you will come to a ruined hut, the Cason di Formin, set in beautiful pastureland. We pick up Route 434, and some more steep bends take us up a wooded ridge and to the grazing grounds on the far northern flanks of Croda da Lago. Bear right on the eastern side of the massif and come to a wide plateau; then head south — towards the Becco di Mezzodi — to reach the lake. The shelter lies on its left bank. The Becco di Mezzodi, shown in the photograph above, is known as 'Cortina's Clock'.

Return □ The return walk follows the same route.

Approach: Cortina d'Ampezzo (1211m/3970ft), a popular international tourist centre in the upper Boite Valley

Starting point/parking: Passo Tre Croci (1805m), a pass between Cristallo and the Sorapis Group, accessible by car or by bus from Cortina (9km)

Overnight suggestions: Hotel Tre Croci (1805m, private, open from the beginning of July until the end of August, 200 beds); or the Vandelli Shelter (1928m, run by the Venice branch of the Italian Alpine Club, open from 20 June until 20 September, 38 beds, 22 bunks)

Walking time: from the Passo Tre Croci to the Vandelli Shelter about 1h30min–1h45min; the return about 45min–1h; *total time 2h15min–2h45min*

Grade: an easy walk, but note that you must be sure-footed and accustomed to heights!

Highest point: Vandelli Shelter (1928m/6325ft), reached after a *climb of 123m/405ft*

Best time of year: end of June until the end of September

The semicircular Sorapis Basin ('Circo di Sorapis'), surrounded by high rock walls, is one of the sights of the Misurina area. Up in this circle of rock stands the Vandelli Shelter, a meeting-point for the mountain-climbing fraternity and a highly-recommended overnight base. This shelter can be reached on foot from the Tre Croci Pass via a footpath commanding very good

The Sorapis Group from the Misurina Lake in the north

16

views — especially towards the northern Dolomites, including Cristallo, the Drei Zinnen, and the Cadini di Misurina. Once you reach the shelter, you'll want to spend some time beside little Lake Sorapis — beneath the forbidding walls of the Tre Sorelle, the Punta Sorapis and the bold, lofty pinnacle called 'God's Finger' (Dito di Dio). Let the magic landscape of this rock amphitheatre cast its spell over you. . . .

From the Tre Croci Pass to the Vandelli Shelter □ From the pass, walk along the Great Dolomite Road in the direction of Misurina for about 200 metres (yards). You'll see a fork to the right; it is a signposted cart-track (Route 215) and part of the 'High-Level Route' 3. Follow it gently uphill, heading southeast, until it ends at a steep escarpment. Here continue on a footpath and follow it to the right into a little valley, which is circled to the left. On leaving it, head east through a wood, climbing to the saddle between Col Cucco and the Cime di Malquoira. Continue on even ground through forest, heading southeast, until the path bears right (south) and makes for the Val Sorapis. On leaving the forest you climb steeply to a saddle and then follow the rocky eastern flanks of the Cime di Laudo (rock stairway, wire ropes). In somewhat gentler surroundings, cross the river and bear left to the shelter.

The return □ The return follows the same route.

Approach: Cortina d'Ampezzo (1211m/3970ft), a popular international tourist centre in the upper Boite Valley

Parking/funicular: Park at the Miètres chair lift station in Verocai (1.5km from the centre of Cortina). Take the chair lift to the Miètres Shelter.

Starting point: Miètres Shelter (1710m), at the top of the second section of the chair lift

Overnight suggestion: Hotel Tre Croci (1805m, private, open from the beginning of July until the end of August, 200 beds); you can also get refreshments at the Miètres Shelter (1710m, private, restaurant, but no overnight accommodation offered).

Walking time: from the Miètres Shelter to the Passo Sonforca (ascent) about 2h15min; from the Passo Sonforca to the Passo Tre Croci (descent) about 30—45min; *total time about 2h45min—3h*

Grade: The route follows a steep ridge on the ascent to the Zumèles Saddle; **surefootedness and a head for heights are necessary. Take extra care in wet weather!**

Highest point: Passo Sonforca (2130m/6985ft), reached after a *climb of 400m/1310ft*

Best time of year: mid-June until mid-September

Hint: From the Passo Sonforca climb up another 100m/325ft to the Sonforca Shelter (2215m, private, open from the beginning of July until the end of September, 25 beds).

***T**he southern flanks of the Pomagagnon Group near Cortina are very popular with walkers. One of the best excursions you can tackle is the climb up to the Sonforca Pass — the gateway to the higher Cristallo Group. From this walk you will have a marvellous outlook over Cortina's basin and the mighty Dolomites surrounding the town. The walk finishes with a

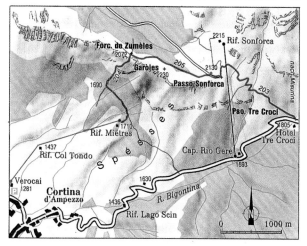

descent to the Tre Croci Pass, from where you can catch a bus back to Cortina.

From the Mièment Shelter to the Passo Sonforca via the Zumèles Saddle ▫

From the Mièment Shelter to the Passo Sonforca via the Zumèles Saddle ▫

Follow the footpath (waymarked in red), going through a larch wood and heading northwest to a meadow, where there is a cross-track (and a signpost). Go right — northeast — on the track (Route 204) through dwarf pines and larch, to climb to the edge of the forest. From here you climb straight up over pastureland and then bear right towards a ridge. Zig-zag up a path to cross it and, finally, go through a craggy gulley to the Zumèles Saddle (2072m). On the other side, you follow Route 205 east (right) through a beautiful stand of stone pines — from where there are wonderful views of Cristallo. It's a gentle descent to the Sonforca Pass, lying between the Cristallo Group in the north and Pomagagnon in the south. From here take Route 203 on the southern ridges of Cristallo, to go through woods and over pastureland southeast to an unsurfaced road, which is followed to the Tre Croci Pass.

Opposite: the Tofana Group is seen to the west

Approach: Cortina d'Ampezzo (1211m/3970ft), a very popular tourist centre in the upper Boite Valley

Parking/funicular: Park at the station for the Col de Varda chair lift at the southeast end of Lake Misurina (1752m). You can get there by car or by bus from Cortina (15km) or Schluderbach (7km). Take the chair lift to the Col de Varda Shelter.

Starting point: Col de Varda Shelter (2115m), at the upper end of the chair lift

Overnight suggestions: Col de Varda Shelter (2115m, private, open from 1 July to 20 September, 20 beds, 10 bunks); or Città di Carpi shelter (2110m, run by the Carpi branch of the Italian Alpine Club, open from 1 July until 20 September, 30 bunks)

Walking time: from the Col de Varda Shelter to the viewpoint (Forcella Maraia) about 1h30min; the return about 1h30min; *total time 3h*

Grade: a very easy walk on well-signposted tracks and unsurfaced roads

Highest point: Col de Varda Shelter (2115m/6935ft); this is reached by the chair lift, and the *walk is on level terrain for the most part*

Best time of year: beginning of June until the end of September

Hint: From the Città di Carpi Shelter, you could walk down to the Hotel Cristallo in Federavecchia (Route 120, part of the Dolomite 'High-Level Route' 4). This is a descent of 727m/2385ft, and takes about 1h30min. From the hotel you can get a bus back to Misurina.

The Città di Carpi Shelter below the Cadin Group

20

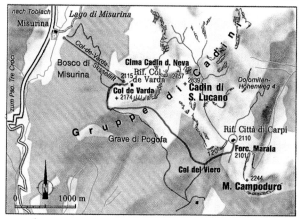

Misurina is the starting point for this excursion, which visits two splendidly-situated mountain shelters. A Dolomite 'high-level' road takes us from the Col de Varda around the south side of the Cadin della Neve peak, to the Città di Carpi Shelter near the viewpoint called 'Forcella Maraia'. From the alpine meadows at this little-known belvedere not only will you have a superb outlook towards the central peaks of the Cadin Group, but an equally fantastic view south to the heights of Marmarole and Sorapis.

From the Col de Varda Shelter to the Forcella Maraia and the Città di Carpi Shelter □

Follow the unsurfaced road heading west for about 200m (yards), descending to a fork. Here go left on a well-signposted mountain cart-track (Route 120, part of the Dolomite 'High-Level Route' 4). You will make a leftward arc around the Col de Varda and then round the south side of Cadin della Neve. Then, heading southeast through pines and a sprinkling of larch woods, you'll descend to a 'corner'. On meeting a fork, follow the Route 116 waymarking (red paint) to the left, climbing northeast to the lovely larch-wooded meadows and the Forcella Maraia.

The return □ Follow the same route back.

Approach: Cortina d'Ampezzo (1211m/3970ft), a popular international tourist centre in the upper Boite Valley

Starting point/parking: Misurina (1752m), a broad green plateau (with a well-known lake, see Walk 5), located between the Cristallo Group in the west and the Cadin Group in the east. Misurina is accessible by car or bus from Cortina (15km) or Schluderbach (7km).

Overnight suggestions: There are several hotels in Misurina; otherwise the Fonda Savio Shelter (2367m, run by the Trieste branch of the Italian Alpine Club, open from mid-June until the end of September, 24 beds, 25 bunks)

Walking time: from Misurina to the Fonda Savio Shelter about 1h30min; the return about 45min—1h; *total time under 2h30min*

Grade: fairly strenuous climbing, but not difficult

Highest point: Fonda Savio Shelter (2367m/7765ft), reached after a *climb of 615m/2015ft*

Best time of year: mid-June until mid-October

Misurina boasts a great variety of walks that are both straightforward and easily accessible by car or bus. The route described here visits an extremely pleasant little shelter located on the wild and rocky heights of the Passo dei Tocci in the centre of the Cadin Group. This mountain refuge is frequented by both high-level walkers (the Dolomite 'High-Level Route' 4 passes it) and climbers. This walk is a lot easier than any *they* are tackling, even if it is one of the most strenuous in this book! Your reward will be wonderful views of the Cristallo Group and the Hohe Gaisl in the west and northwest.

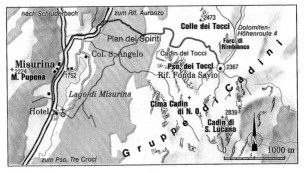

The Cadin Group seen from the northwest

From Misurina to the Fonda Savio Shelter via the Cadin dei Tocci □

From the lovely Misurina Lake (see Walk 5), follow the Great Dolomite Road north to the right-hand fork to the Auronzo Shelter (signposted). Fork right here, to head northeast. You will come to another fork: keep right for the Auronzo Shelter. After some 500 metres (yards) another fork is reached, where an old military road (Route 115) branches off to the right. Follow it east through woods to the Pian degli Spiriti, a plateau at 1880m, where there is a parking area and a lift for provisioning the Savio Shelter. From here follow the cart-track over the mostly green terrain. You're heading east uphill in the Cadin dei Tocci combe. You'll climb it on the left-hand side all the way up to the Tocci Pass and the shelter.

The return □ The descent follows the same route.

Approach: Cortina d'Ampezzo (1211m/3970ft), a popular international tourist centre in the upper Boite Valley, or Schluderbach (1438m/4715ft), a grouping of hotels in the upper Höhlenstein Valley

Starting point/parking: Auronzo Shelter (2320m), above the Longères Saddle, accessible by car or bus from Cortina (23km) or Schluderbach (15km). The approach is via Misurina, from where there is a toll road (8km) to the shelter and its very large parking area.

Overnight suggestions: Auronzo Shelter (2333m, run by the Cadorina branch of the Italian Alpine Club, open from the beginning of June until the end of September, 60 beds); or the Drei Zinnen Shelter (2405m, run by the Padova branch of the Italian Alpine Club, open from mid-June until the end of September, 100 beds, 100 bunks)

Walking time: from the Auronzo Shelter to the Patern Saddle and on to the Drei Zinnen Shelter 1h15min–1h30min; from the Drei Zinnen Shelter to the Col di Mezzo Saddle and on to the Auronzo Shelter 1h45min–2h; *total time about 3h–3h30min*

Grade: an easy, well-signposted circular walk

Highest point: Patern Saddle (2454m/8050ft), reached after a short climb. *(Total climb en route 250m/820ft)*

Best time of year: beginning of July until the end of September

The Drei Zinnen – the 'Three Pinnacles' – are famous landmarks in the Dolomites. This setting is a magnet attracting not only walkers and climbers, but anyone enjoying a

The Drei Zinnen, with the shelter of the same name

24

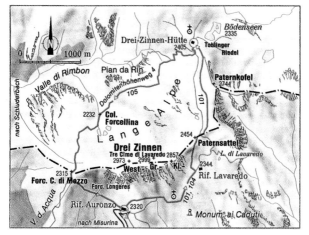

motoring holiday. Thanks to the toll road from Misurina, everyone can walk to the Patern Saddle and marvel at the fantastic outlook towards the famous north walls (seen in the photograph opposite). But don't leave it at that! Complete the circuit, visit the shelter and carry on via the Col di Mezzo; that way you'll see the 'Three Pinnacles' from all angles!

To the Drei Zinnen Shelter via the Patern Saddle □ Follow the wide track (Route 101) along the scree-covered southern slopes of the pinnacles, aiming for the Lavaredo Shelter. Just before reaching it, head left (north) over rubble, and climb steeply up to the Patern Saddle. Beyond it, you'll cross scree fields on the western slopes of the Paternkopfel and descend to the shelter.

To the Auronzo Shelter via the Col di Mezzo □ Follow Route 101 south to a fork and here go right on Route 105, crossing meadows. Head down west to the fork at the steep drop towards the Rimbon Valley. Here go left (south) over the flat pastures of the Pian da Rin and up to the Langen Alpe Plateau, which is crossed by heading southwest. More rubble comes underfoot at the Col di Mezzo Saddle; on the other side of it, bear left (southeast) over the scree to descend.

Approach: San Vito di Cadore (1011m/3610ft), a popular international tourist centre in the middle of the Boite Valley

Starting point/parking: Zoppa Bar (1429m), 3km from San Vito; accessible by car only

Overnight suggestion: San Marco Shelter (1823m, run by the Venice branch of the Italian Alpine Club, open from 20 June until 30 September, 30 beds, 10 bunks)

Walking time: from the Bar Zoppa to the San Marco Shelter about 1h15min; the return about 45min; *total time 2h*

Grade: a straightforward climb on good tracks and paths

Highest point: San Marco Shelter (1823m/5980ft), reached after a *climb of 394m/1290ft*

Best time of year: mid-June until the end of September

For connoisseurs of beautifully-situated alpine shelters with splendid views: here's a dainty morsel for you to sample! It's the Rifugio San Marco, set under the southern walls of the Belpra (Marmarole Group), on the shoulder of the Col dechi da Os. Sitting up here — high over the Boite Valley, facing the grandiose mass of Mount Pelmo, and with the Antelao 'within arm's reach — you feel as if you're looking at a

theatrical setting created by Nature. You will be intoxicated by the spectacle. You may forget the time . . . and forget, too, that nothing on earth lasts forever.

From the Zoppa Bar to the San Marco Shelter □ Take the gravel road (Route 228) that follows the right-hand side of the wide rubble-strewn walls protruding from the southern flanks of the Marmarole Group. The way sweeps up in large curves through dwarf pines to the Rifugio Scotter (1561m, a ski lift station). There's a fork off to the right here, where Route 229 heads northeast to the Galassi Shelter. We keep to the gravel road, crossing the scree-covered slopes, where the odd flecks of green begin to appear. The climb continues as a wide arc is made to the left (northwest). We pass under the hill, the Col dechi da Os. From here the route heads due west on a good path, which curves steeply up through woods to the shelter.

The return □ Follow the same route to descend.

Opposite: San Vito di Cadore, with the Sorapis Group in the background

Approach: Calalzo (806m/2645ft), an international tourist centre at the confluence of the Oten and Piave valleys, with both a bus and a rail station

Starting point/parking: Ponte Rio Diassa (1133m), a bridge in the middle of the Oten Valley, accessible by car (6km from Calalzo)

Overnight suggestion: Chiggiato Shelter (1911m, run by the Venice branch of the Italian Alpine Club, open from the beginning of July until the middle of October, 40 beds)

Walking time: from the Ponte Rio Diassa to the Col Negro about 2h30min; the return between 1h–1h15min; *total time 3h–3h45min*

Grade: a straightforward, but strenuous, climb which should be tackled before mid-day

Highest point: Col Negro (1952m/6400ft), reached after a *climb of 819m/2685ft*

Best time of year: beginning of June until the end of October

O f an abiding loveliness – like Sleeping Beauty, pure and pristine – that's how the Marmarole Group reveals itself to the walker approaching from the south. The climb described here, which takes us from the lovely Val d'Oten up to Col Negro, is quite strenuous, but perfectly safe and straightforward. Right underneath the peak, in the most perfect setting, sits the Chiggiato Shelter, and from this high

point the views are really astounding. You look out at the 1000m-high walls of the central Marmarole in the north, the mighty pyramid of Antelao in the southwest, the spiky crown of the southernmost Karnisch Alps in the east and southeast. There is no more wonderful panorama in all the Dolomites!

From the Rio Diassa Bridge to the Col Negro via the Chiggiato Shelter □
If you're approaching from Calalzo, the track up to the Chiggiato Shelter branches off to the right some 50m (yards) before the bridge over the Rio Diassa. Follow it (the number is Route 260) along the right-hand side of the narrow Diassa Valley, heading north. You reach a fork: bear right and first cross over a steep band of rubble; after this you'll be on a very good footpath that zigzags east uphill through a wonderful forest. After a short stretch of even terrain (where you curve to the left), you climb through more woods up to the refuge. From here the footpath continues east uphill to the highest point in the walk, the 'Black Hill' (Col Negro).

The descent □ Follow the same route to return.

Opposite: the Chiggiato Shelter, beautifully situated above the inner Oten Valley

Approach: Forno di Zoldo (840m/2755ft), a summer resort midway up the Val Zoldana, or Venas di Cadore (558m/1830ft), a resort in the Boite Valley

Starting point/parking: Passo Cibiana (1530m), a pass between the Pelmo and Bosconero Groups, reached by private transport only (from Forno di Zoldo 11km, from Venas di Cadore 9km)

Overnight suggestion: the Remauro Shelter (1530m, private, closed from February until April, otherwise always open, 8 beds)

Walking time: from the Cibiana Pass to the Forcella (Saddle) de le Ciavazole about 1h15min−1h30min; the return about 45min−1h; *total time between 2h−2h 30min*

Grade: This is a very straightforward climb on a well-marked footpath

Highest point: Forcella de le Ciavazole (1994m/6540ft), reached after a *climb of 464m/1520ft*

Best time of year: mid-June until the end of October

Hint: From the western shoulder of Mount Sfornioi there is a wonderful panorama. You can get there from the Ciavazole Saddle in about 30−45min; it's easy going.

The far-reaching views you have on Walk 14 (Mount Rite) are seen again − but this time close up − from the Ciavazole Saddle to the south. You have a fine outlook on the mighty central massif of the Bosconero Group. Even as you are climbing, the panorama spreads before you: Civetta, Pelmo, Sorapis and Antelao. And then − when you reach your goal, the mountain gap − a wonderful tableau greets you: the Sasso di Toanella and Rocchetta Alta di Bosconero peaks, rising on the other side of the Bosconero Valley. This landscape is one of the 'masterpieces' of the southern Alps.

From the Cibiana Pass to the Forcella de le Ciavazole □
Follow the pass road west for some 50m (yards), making for Forno di Zoldo. You'll come to an unsurfaced road branching off left (signposted). Follow it through a larch forest to a fork, where there is another signpost. Go left (south) uphill for 100m (yards), to where the road turns left. Here you will find a well-signposted foot-path (the Dolomite 'High-Level Route' 3). It goes straight ahead (south) through the wood-lands and scrub on the eastern slopes of the Spitz de Copada. You will come to more sign-posts when you reach a pastureland basin on your right. Take the middle route; it's a foot-path marked with orange paint (Route 485). This follows the left-hand edge of the pasture gently uphill, heading left (southeast) up the little valley that terminates where the walk also ends. You climb steeply up the verdant right-hand side of the valley to the Forcella de le Ciavazole, an impressive rock 'gateway' between the Cima Pala Anziana on your right and Mount Sfornioi on your left.

The descent □ Follow the same route to return.

The Bosconero Group from the north

Approach: Domegge di Cadore (763m/2500ft), a village lying above the Centro di Cadore Lake to the west, in the Piave Valley

Starting point/parking: Padova Shelter (1278m, in the upper Talagona Valley, accessible by car from Domegge (9km)

Overnight suggestions: Padova Shelter (1278m, run by the Padova branch of the Italian Alpine Club, open from 20 June until 15 September, and the rest of the year on weekends only, 54 bunks); or the Tita Barba Shelter (1821m, private, open from 20 June until 20 September, and throughout the year on weekends, 16 bunks). You can also obtain refreshments at the Casera Vedorcia (1704m, private, with various dairy products), but there are no overnight facilities.

Walking time: from the Padova Shelter to the Costa di Vedorcia about 2h–2h15min; the return about 1h30min –1h45min; *total time between 3h30min–4h*

Grade: a straightforward, well-signposted climb

Highest point: Capanna Tita Barba, a hut at 1821m/ 5970ft, reached after a *climb of 543m/1780ft*

Best time of year: mid-June until the end of October

---

*S*ome areas lying beyond the Piave Valley in the towering southern Karnisch Alps are geological examples of the purest dolomitic rock. You must be sure to visit them! Walk 13 would take you there, as well as the excursion suggested here, which makes for the Costa di Vedorcia, a high-lying western ridge. This is a relatively little-known, but marvellous viewpoint, from where you can look out to the central Dolomites in the west, as well as the jagged peaks in the east — Cridola, Monfalconi and the Spalti-di-Toro Group.

The Tita Barba Shelter on the Costa di Vedorcia

From the Padova Shelter to the Tita Barba Shelter on the Costa di Vedorcia □
Take Route 350 on the right-hand side of the 'Pra di Toro', a meadow, and head south. Then go right into the forest, from where the way heads southwest towards the northern flanks of the Coll'Alto (where there is a hut). On the other side of this hill, we continue through woodlands down to the Torrente Talagona. Across the stream, it's a short climb up to the Casera Valle, another hut, where there is a fork in the trail. Keep right (west) through larch woods and scrub, first going steeply up towards the Costa di Vedorcia, then making a long curve up to the left — southwest. Finally, larch-studded pasture-lands are crossed in a northwesterly direction, before we reach the balcony-like Casera Vedorcia at 1704m, with its stupendous views towards Cridola, Monfalconi and Spalti-di-Toro. From here a cart-track takes us over meadows and through a sprinkling of larch trees, as we follow the wide curves up to the ridge (the 'Costa' di Vedorcia) and the beautifully-situated Tita Barba Shelter.

The descent □ Follow the same route to return.

Approach: Forni di Sopra (901m/2955ft), a summer resort in the upper Tagliamento Valley, or Lorenzago di Cadore (883m/2895ft), a resort in the Piave Valley

Starting point/parking: Passo della Mauria (1298m), a pass breaching the northern and southern Karnisch Alps. This is accessible by car or by bus from Lorenzago (8km) or Forni di Sopra (9km).

Overnight suggestion: none, but you can obtain refreshments at the Ristorante Passo Mauria.

Walking time: from the Passo della Mauria to the Casere Stabie about 45min; the return between 30—45min; *total time under 1h30min*

Grade: a very easy walk with hardly any climbing

Highest point: Casera Stabie, an upland hut at 1373m/4505ft, reached after a *climb of 75m/245ft*

Best time of year: all year round

___

C lose by *the* Dolomites (if one were to define their geographical position exactly), there are some areas on their perimeter that from a *geological* point of view are just as interesting — if not more so! Among these areas are the Brenta Group west of thè Etschtal and the

area explored in this walk — the southern Karnisch Alps east of the Piave Valley. No matter how splendid the Brenta Group with its colossal formations, here on the east side of the Piave you will find something even more exciting: vertical pillars seemingly made of filigreed rock — a

fantastic labyrinth of towering pinnacles beside which those in the central Dolomites pale in comparison! If you want to take a first look at this area, try Walk 12 if you're feeling energetic. If, on the other hand, you're after a lazy day, but you still want to capture fantastic views and fill your lungs with alpine air, try this short foray over larch-dotted meadows to the Casera Stabie, a little hut north of the Mauria Pass. *Do* pack a picnic, even though this is a very short walk, because you will want to spend the whole day admiring the views towards the Cridola and Monfalconi 'spires' shown opposite.

From the Passo della Mauria to the Casera Stabie □ Take the gently undulating footpath from the pass to the point where it crosses a narrow road. Follow this to the right (east) as far as the saddle between the Colle Famazzo and the Cima Vente — it's all on the flat. From this saddle, the road bends to the left and heads into the Torrente Stabia Valley. Follow it along the eastern slopes of the Cima Vente to penetrate the valley and reach the wonderful meadows around the Casere Stabie, a haymaking-hut.

The return □ Go back the way you came.

Opposite: the Cridola Group and the Casera Stabie

Approach: Forno di Zoldo (840m/2755ft), an international tourist centre in the Zoldana Valley, or Venas di Cadore (558m/1830ft), a holiday centre in the Boite Valley

Starting point/parking: Park at the Cibiana Pass (1530m) between the Pelmo and Bosconero mountains, accessible by car from Forno di Zoldo (11km) or Venas de Cadore (9km)

Overnight suggestion: Remauro Shelter at the Cibiana Pass (1530m, private, closed from February to April, but otherwise always open, 8 beds)

Walking time: Cibiana Pass to Mount Rite about 2h; the return about 1h—1h15min; *total time about 3h*

Grade: an uncomplicated climb along an old military road. An early start is recommended; the route is very sunny!

Highest point: Mount Rite (2183m/7160ft), reached after a *climb of 653m/2140ft*

Best time of year: mid-June until the beginning of November

Passo Cibiana, with its well-run shelter, is a good jumping-off point for this expedition in a little-known area of the Dolomites. Our goal is the easily-reached Mount Rite, north of the pass. Rising in splendid isolation between the Boite, Maè and Piave valleys, this mostly-

verdant mountain commands a setting of such strategic significance that Italy mounted fortifications here during the war in the Dolomites (1915-18). From the summit, the views all round are fantastic.

This panorama encompasses Bosconero in the south, Schiara and the Prampèr Dolomites in the southwest, Civetta-Moiazza in the west, Pelmo in the northwest, Marmolada, Nuvolau, Croda da Lago, Tofana, Fanes and Sorapis in the north, and Antelao and the Karnish Alps in the northeast and east!

From the Cibiana Pass to Mount Rite □
From the Remauro Shelter follow the narrow unsurfaced road (Route 479) along the lightly-wooded southern inclines of the mountain, making for an escarpment. Below this, head left (west) and through a tunnel. On the other side you will come to a ruined military building. The way now heads northwest over pastureland, winding up to the Deona Pass (2053m) between Coll'Alto on the left and Mount Rite on the right. From here there is a stupendous view towards the Dolomite massif north of the Boite Valley. The way curves to the right to follow the southern flanks of the mountain up to more ruined military buildings, from where a few more curves take us to the summit. While marvelling at the views, watch out for the old shafts in the battlements up here!

The return □ The map indicates a steep shortcut that you might use to descend.

Opposite: Antelao, one of many peaks seen from Mt Rite

Approach: Pescul (1415m/4640ft), a resort in the Fiorentina Valley with a superb outlook to Mount Pelmo

Starting point/parking: Park at the upper end of the Fiorentina Valley (1663m), by the fork-off to the Città di Fiume Shelter. Note: parking space is limited.

Overnight suggestions: Città di Fiume Shelter (1950m, run by the Fiume branch of the Italian Alpine Club, open from 10 June until 25 September, 26 beds); or Passo Staulanza Shelter (1766m, private, open from mid-June until the end of September, 20 beds)

Walking time: from the end of the Fiorentina Valley to the Città di Fiume Shelter about 1h30min; from the Città di Fiume Shelter to the Passo Staulanza Shelter about 1h30min; from the Passo Staulanza Shelter back to the starting point some 30min; *total time 3h30min*

Grade: an easy circuit on well-signposted trails

Highest point: Città di Fiume Shelter (1950m/6395ft), reached after a *climb of 255m/835ft*

Best time of year: beginning of June until the end of October

I f you haven't seen Mount Pelmo rising above the Fiorentina Valley, you don't know the Dolomites! It's a giant of fantastic proportions. Its mass, position and shape all contribute to beautify the entire surroundings. The walk described here starts at the end of the Fiorentina

Valley and takes us first to the Città di Fiume Shelter, from where there are marvellous views. You can take a rest here before setting off again to follow the splendid path under Pelmo's northern escarpment and over to the Staulanza Pass, from where a short descent along the asphalted Staulanza road takes you back to the starting point.

From the end of the Fiorentina Valley to the Città di Fiume Shelter □
Branch off from the local road (No 251) at the 1663m marker, following the unsurfaced road (Route 467, signposted). You head north via the Malga Fiorentina, a meadowland hut, and up to the shelter.

From the Città di Fiume Shelter to the Staulanza Pass □
Take the footpath (Route 472, part of the Dolomite 'High-Level Route' 1) south through dwarf pines and continue until you are below a saddle, the Forcella Forada. Here head right (southwest) to follow the scree- and rock-strewn northern walls of Mount Pelmo. Passing through a wood, come to a fork and a signpost: head right here, to descend to the pass.

The return (descent) into the Val Fiorentina □
Follow the northern side of the asphalted road to curve down to the viewpoint where you set off.

Opposite: the Civetta Group from the Staulanza Pass

Approach: Forno di Zoldo (840m/2755ft), a tourist centre halfway up the Zoldana Valley, from where there are many nearby excursions

Starting point/parking: Zoppe di Cadore (1460m), a mountain village on the south side of Mount Pelmo in the Torto Valley (an offshoot of the Zoldana Valley). Zoppe di Cadore is accessible by car or by bus from Forno di Zoldo (9km).

Overnight suggestions: There are several guesthouses in Zoppe di Cadore; otherwise the Venezia Shelter (1947m, run by the Venice branch of the Italian Alpine Club, open from 20 June until 20 September, 32 beds, 40 bunks).

Walking time: from Zoppe di Cadore to the Venezia Shelter about 1h30min−2h; the return about 45min−1h; *total time under 3h*

Grade: a straightforward climb on well-signposted tracks

Highest point: Sella di Rutorto, a saddle at 1950m/6395ft, reached after a *climb of 490m/1605ft*

Best time of year: early June until the end of October

The little-known outlook towards the southern side of Mount Pelmo is just as beautiful as that towards its northern slopes. However, you can only capture these views from the lonely heights of the southern Dolomites around Zoldo. At the foot of Pelmo's giant southern escarpment you will find a multitude of

side-valleys cradling dreamy little hamlets — of which Zoppe di Cadore is the most lovely. From here you can take an easy walk to the Venezia Shelter, situated on the eastern rim of Mount Pelmo. This climb affords the walker splendid, far-reaching views over to the south, to the Bosconero, Prampèr, Tàmer and Moiazza groups. And then, when we reach the

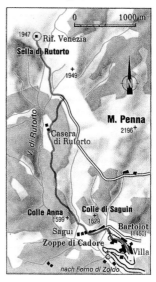

Rutorto Saddle at 1950m, the northern Dolomites on the far side of the Boite Valley also come into view.

From Zoppe di Cadore to the Venezia Shelter via the Sella di Rutorto □

Leave Zoppe di Cadore by heading west on the road. You will come to a cart-track branching off right (Route 471, signposted). Follow it in a westerly direction through woodlands; the way is mostly even walking. You will later bear right in a gulley, where there is a fork and a crucifix. On the other side of the gulley, cross meadows and go through a light larch wood, heading up northwest to the Colle Anna, a ridge that climbs north towards Mount Penna. Cross the ridge and come to another cart-track crossing yours; head left on it, into the broad pastureland basin under the southeastern outcrops of Mount Pelmo. From here curve up north to the Rutorto Saddle and from there go gently down to the shelter.

The return □ Take the same route to return.

Opposite: Mount Pelmo from the southeast

Approach: Fusine (1177m/3860ft), in the upper Zoldana Valley

Starting point/parking: Costa (1425m), a hamlet on the southern inclines of Mount Pelmo. Costa is located in a side-valley and is only accessible by car, via narrow mountain roads (2km from Fusine). Note: parking space is limited.

Overnight suggestion/refreshments: none

Walking time: from Costa to Monte Punta about 1h 15min−1h30min; the return about 45min−1h; *total time 2h−2h30min*

Grade: a fairly strenuous, but not difficult, climb on good trails. **Note: there is no waymarking.**

Highest point: Monte Punta (1952m/6400ft), reached after a *climb of 527m/1730ft*

Best time of year: beginning of June until the end of October

---

A midst the far-reaching lower inclines of Mount Pelmo, isolated rock masses stand out from their surroundings: the 'Giants of the Cadore'. The high lonely peaks here make splendid viewing points, but they are seldom visited. Among these 'giants' is Mount Punta, on the far southern edge of the massif, north of Forno di Zoldo. Its treeless crown can be reached

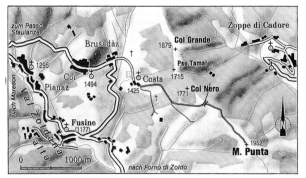

via good (but unwaymarked) trails from the upper Zoldana Valley — without too much huffing and puffing! Once you are up on the saddle of the mountain, just at the centre of the Dolomites around Zoldo, you will overlook a great part of this fascinating mountain world.

From Costa to Monte Punta via the northwest ridge □
From the fountain in Costa climb up the steep stone footpath, heading east. You reach the crossing of a cart-track. Turn right on the track (southeast), and follow the western slopes of the Col Nero over larch-covered meadows. You will reach a fork: bear left on a wide track, to continue in the same direction, first crossing over a steep ridge. Keep heading east: some curves in the track take you to a pastureland saddle (1723m) between Col Nero in the north and Monte Punta in the south. On the shoulder of Mount Punta, bear right up the wooded northwestern ridge on a footpath (or any one of its ramifications), making for the summit. You'll be going up steeply through scrub at first, but later you will cross the grassy ridge on a more gentle incline as you near the peak.

The return □ Follow the same route to descend.

Opposite: the mighty massif of the Civetta, from the east

Approach: Forno di Zoldo (840m/2755ft), a tourist centre from where you can embark on any number of excursions in the middle of the Zoldana Valley

Starting point/parking: Forno di Zoldo

Overnight suggestion: none, but you can obtain refreshments at the restaurant at Pralongo.

Walking time: Forno di Zoldo to Colcerver about 1h; the return about 45min; *total time 1h45min*

Grade: a straightforward walk along roads

Highest point: Colcerver (1221m/4005ft), reached after a *climb of 381m/1250ft*

Best time of year: possible all year round, but at its most beautiful in early summer and autumn

---

Forno di Zoldo is a little known holiday area, yet it's as good a centre from which to make excursions in the northern Dolomites as any of the larger and better-known villages — perhaps even better. Near Forno are some truly delightful hamlets — 'showplaces' for the area. One of the most attractive is the tiny settlement of Colcerver, situated on the south side of the Val Zoldana, on the Col Baion. The hamlet is worth a visit not only because of the interesting approach to it and its location high above the Zoldo and Pramprèr valleys, but also for the little-known — but absolutely fabulous — view you'll have towards the rock towers of the Bosconero and Pramprèr groups. The straight-forward walk described here follows a mountain road to visit this 'balcony' settlement, via the lower village of Pralongo.

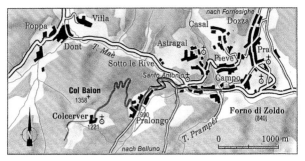

44

The towers of the Spiz di Mezzodi, seen from the north-west

From Forno di Zoldo to Colcerver via Pralongo □ From the centre of Forno, head west towards the Duran Pass by road (number 347). Go as far as St Anthony Church. Here go left (signposted) on an asphalt road and cross the River Maè. You will come to a fork (where there are more signposts). Go right, climbing up through woods to Pralongo, situated at the entrance to the lovely Malisia Valley. From here there are wonderful views towards the Tàmer Group and the towers of the Spiz di Mezzodi (Prampèr Group) in the southeast. We follow a narrow asphalt road out of Pralongo, heading right and curving uphill to the Col Baion, accompanied by a very fine view of Mount Pelmo in the north. A long curve to the left then brings us to the balcony setting of Colcerver, in the meadowlands below the Baion.

The return □ The descent follows the same route.

Approach: Forno di Zoldo (840m/2755ft), a tourist centre from where you can embark on a number of excursions in the middle of the Zoldana Valley

Starting point/parking: Forno di Zoldo

Overnight suggestions/refreshments: none

Walking time: from Forno di Zoldo to the Pian del Palui about 1h30min—1h45min; the return a little over 1h; *total time some 2h30min—3h*

Grade: uncomplicated climb on well-signposted cart-tracks or unsurfaced roads

Highest point: Pian dei Palui (1480m/4855ft), reached after a *climb of 640m/2100ft*

Best time of year: beginning of May until the end of October

Hint: You can extend this walk by going on to the Pramperèt shelter (1857m); this takes another 1h15min each way.

Val Prampèr — a valley running north/south — lies at the centre of the somewhat out-of-the-way, and thus little-visited, Prampèr Dolomites. This valley is, however, one of the most interesting and beautiful in the whole region. Take half a day to explore it! The goal of the walk described here is the Pian dei Palui, a plateau of perfectly flat meadowland overlooked by the fantastic tower-like peaks and

pinnacles of the Spiz di Mezzodì in the northeast. What a wonderful spot! The single shelter in this area — the Rifugio Pramperèt — can be reached from here in just a little over an hour, in case you've lost your heart to the valley and would like to spend the night.

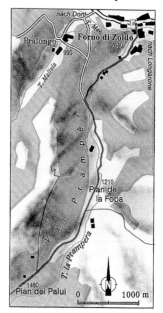

From Forno di Zoldo to the Pian dei Palui □

From the bridge over the Maè in the centre of town (by the Cafè Central), go up between the houses (southwest) and then go left over the Torrente Prampèra. You will come to a fork: go right on a cart-track which climbs gently up through larch-covered meadows. From here there are very good views towards the line of towers comprising the Spiz di Mezzodì and Mount Pelmo. The stream is crossed again, and you head right to an unsurfaced road (Route 523). Join it and head south through woods to a water tank, from where the way curves steeply up to the Pian de la Fopa (1210m). Continue up the valley on the road, bearing right in the wood and then curving westwards to a spring ('Aqua Benedetta'). Finally, go southwest to the Palui Plateau and its scattered conifers — a wonderful Dolomite setting.

The return □ The return follows the same route.

Opposite: the Pian dei Palui, halfway up the Val Prampèr

Approach: Faè/Fortogna (469m/1540ft), two villages in the Piave Valley, on the eastern rim of the Schiara Group

Starting point/parking: Park at the bus/rail station for Faè/Fortogna; it stands about halfway between the two villages, some 14km from Belluno. Also accessible by bus from Belluno

Overnight suggestion: none, but you can obtain refreshments at the Casera di Caiada (1157m, private, a dairy farm open only in the summer).

Walking time: from Faè/Fortogna to the Pian di Caiada about 2h–2h15min; the return about 1h30min–1h 45min; *total time between 3h30min–4h*

Grade: an uncomplicated but quite strenuous climb on well-signposted roads and paths. Note: it can be very hot around mid-day!

Highest point: Casera di Caiada (1157m/3795ft), reached after a *climb of 714m/2340ft*

Best time of year: mid-May until the end of October

Hint: You can go as far as the Pian di Caiada by car on a narrow asphalt road that curves up the left side of the Desedàn Valley from Faè (7km).

The Schiara Group, with its audacious 'iron ladders', is above all the climber's domain. But here and there the walker will find a kinder slope to tackle, and this excursion visits one of them. When you first approach the Val Desedàn, a tributary of the Piave, from the east, as a walker you are likely to be intimidated! The landscape is desolate and chaotic. But once you attain the upper end of the valley, the outlook changes completely: you will find lovely

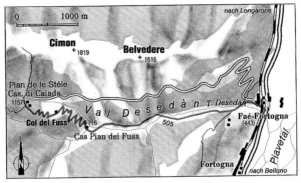

Pian di Caiada, in the Schiara Group

pastureland clothed in firs, as you can see in the photograph above. Beyond rises the mighty Cima di Caiada with its phalanx of 'towers'.

From Faè/Fortogna to the Pian di Caiada via the Val Desedàn □
Take road No 200 from the bus/rail station and head north. Then turn left under the railway and go west over the wide scree belt of the Desedàn Valley, heading up to the boulder-strewn walls at the end of the ravine. From here take the footpath (Route 505), zig-zagging up north. Then head left (northwest) around the southern flanks of the Pala della Stanga. Finally head south across a wide landslip, and you will come to a wooded ridge. Weaving uphill across it in a generally westerly direction, you come to the Pian di Caiada, a fir-studded plateau. There is a small dairy farm here, where you might like to replenish your picnic basket.

The return □ Follow the same route to descend.

Approach: Cortina d'Ampezzo (1211m/3972ft), a popular tourist centre in the upper Boite Valley

Parking/funicular: Park at the station for the Scoiattoli chair lift on the Falzarego Pass road 6km from Cortina. Take the chair lift to the Scoiattoli Shelter.

Starting point: Scoiattoli Shelter (2280m), at the upper end of the chair lift

Overnight suggestions: Scoiattoli Shelter (2280m, private, open from the beginning of July until the end of September, 20 beds); Nuvolau Shelter (2575m, run by the Cortina branch of the Italian Alpine Club, open from the beginning of June until 5 October, 16 beds, 9 bunks); or Averau Shelter (2413m, private, open from the beginning of July until the end of September, 35 beds)

Walking time: from the Scoiattoli Shelter to Mount Nuvolau (ascent) about 1h; from Monte Nuvolau to the Falzarego Pass and on to the chair lift station/parking area (the return) about 2h–2h30min; *total time about 3h–3h30min*

Grade: an easy climb on well-signposted footpaths

Highest point: Monte Nuvolau (2575m/8445ft), reached after a *climb of 295m/965ft*

Best time of year: beginning of June until the end of September

---

Nuvolau and its group, situated between the Falzarego and Giau passes, have many advantages from the walker's point of view — not least of which is the area's accessibility. Almost all the walking bases are reached by car or chair

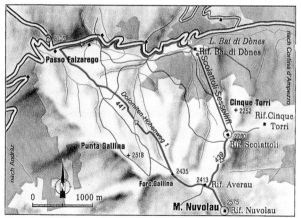

lift, so you can get to the start of the walk very quickly. From the Scoiattoli Shelter (where there are splendid views) there are any number of routes to nearby Monte Nuvolau, all of them safe and heavily-frequented. The route described here is a circular one, and so easy that it should appeal to even the least energetic rambler.

From the Scoiattoli Shelter to Monte Nuvolau □ Either take Route 439 or the unsurfaced road to the right of it, crossing green fields and heading uphill west towards the Nuvolau Saddle, where the Averau Shelter lies below the Nuvolau and Averau peaks. From this shelter cross the north ridge and climb to the summit of Nuvolau and another shelter, run by the Italian Alpine Club.

The return via the Falzarego Pass □ Go back down to the Nuvolau Saddle and there pick up Route 441 below the southern walls of Mount Averau. Follow the way southwest to the Gallina Saddle at 2435m. From here cross another pasture, heading northwest to the Falzarego Pass. Now simply follow the Great Dolomite Road eastwards, down towards Cortina, until you come back to the lower station of the Scoiattoli chair lift.

Opposite: the Nuvolau landscape near the Cinque Torri

Approach: Villagrande (1443m/4735ft), the most important village of the Colle Santa Lucia district, located on an outcropping of Monte Pore high over the Fiorentina Valley

Starting point/parking: Villagrande; park in the main square.

Overnight suggestion: There are several guesthouses and hotels in Villagrande.

Walking time: *1h30min total* for this circular walk

Grade: very easy

Highest point: Canazei (1575m/5165ft), reached after a *climb of 132m/430ft*

Best time of year: possible all year round, but at its best in the autumn, when the leaves are changing colour

There are some Alpine settings that are so perfect in their beauty and harmony that to walk through them is almost to commit trespass. Among these tableaux spring to mind the Dachstein from the Gosau Lake, the Sciora and Badile groups from Soglio, and of course the Matterhorn from Zermatt. Another of these unforgettable landscapes is the setting of Villa-

grande, at the entrance to the Fiorentina Valley. The hilltop church leads the eye up the lovely pastureland of the valley to the peaks of Mount Pelmo, one of the most spectacular crests in the Dolomites. The walk described here draws us into this perfectly harmonious tapestry.

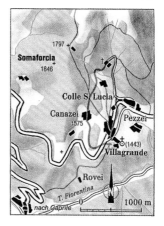

Circular walk from Villagrande to Canazei and Ru, then back to Villagrande □

From the main square in the village head left to pass by the Hotel Post. From there follow the wide track westwards over meadowland and through a light sprinkling of larch trees, to climb steeply up the southern inclines of Mount Pore. This ridge is crossed on a cart-track, and we bear right uphill to the hamlet of Canazei. From here we follow a road on the eastern side of the ridge and head northeast in a forest to the farmsteads of Ru (1534m). Just beyond here, the gulley of the Rio Pavia streambed is reached. Bear sharp right (south) through the gulley and make for the crossing of the road (No 251) below. Follow the road in a southerly direction, going gently uphill and back to Villagrande.

Opposite: the perfect setting of Villagrande, with Mount Pelmo in the background

Approach: Pescul (1415m/4640ft), or Pecol (1382m/4530ft), health resorts in the upper Fiorentina and Zoldana valleys

Starting point/parking: Passo Staulanza (see also Walk 21); this pass is 7km from Pescul or 8km from Pecol and accessible by car or by bus.

Overnight suggestion: Passo Staulanza Shelter (1766m, private, open from mid-June until the end of September, 20 beds, see photograph Walk 21). You can also obtain refreshments at Malga Vescovà (1722, a private dairy farm), but there are no overnight facilities there.

Walking time: from the Staulanza Pass to Malga Vescovà about 45min; the return about 45min; *total time 1h30min*

Grade: very easy; mostly on level terrain

Highest point: Passo Staulanza (1766m/5790ft)

Best time of year: all year round

Hint: If you feel energetic, why not climb to the green summit of the Roa Bianca, from where there are some fine views. The footpath is just south of Malga Vescovà and well-signposted. It will take about 45min to climb this peak (238m/780ft).

If you would like to see the colossus of Mount Pelmo from a different, less well-known angle, then this walk can be highly recommended; it's easy, too! The route takes us to the Malga Vescovà, a little hut on the northern side of the Civetta Group, in the Rio Canedo side-valley. You can get there on foot or by bicycle. The hut is accessible by car as well, but that is *not* the recommended approach! On your excursion you

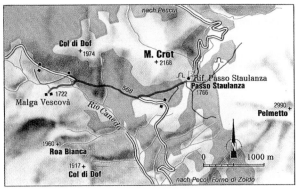

Mount Pelmo from Malga Vescovà

will enjoy wonderful views over the sub-alpine
Mount Fernazza, set between the Civetta Group
and Mount Pelmo. If you have time, do climb up
the nearby Roa Bianca, from where not only
will you have fabulous views of Mount Pelmo,
but also unexpected outlooks to the little-known
areas around the Prampèr and Tàmer in the south.

From the Passo Staulanza to the Malga Vescovà □
Take the wide asphalt road (No 251) west towards Pecol. After about 1km downhill, come to
the first curve to the left. Here bear right on an
unsurfaced road (Route 568) to follow the
right-hand side of the Canedo Valley. Passing
through woods and over meadows, head west up
the valley to a fork (signposted). Going downhill
half-left, cross the Rio Canedo and then mount
the opposite bank to climb up to the Malga
Vescovà, where there is a small dairy farm.

The return □ Follow the same route back.

Approach: Pecol (1382m/4530ft), a summer resort in the upper Zoldana Valley

Starting point/parking: Forcella d'Alleghe (1816m), a saddle on the north side of the central Civetta Group between Monte Coldai and the Roa Bianca. To get there from Pecol, take the Staulanza Pass road to Palafavera and there turn left (signposted) on an unsurfaced road to the saddle (7km from Pecol).

Overnight suggestion: Coldai Shelter (2132m, run by the Venice branch of the Italian Alpine Club, open from mid-June until the end of September, 50 beds, 30 bunks). You can also obtain refreshments at the Forcella d'Alleghe Bar (1816m, private, open in the summer only).

Walking time: from the Forcella d'Alleghe to the Coldai Shelter about 45min—1h; the return about 30min; *total time between 1h15min—1h30min*

Grade: straightforward climb on a well-signposted cart-track

Highest point: Coldai Shelter (2132m/6990ft), reached after a *climb of 316m/1035ft*

Hint: It's well worth while to make the short climb west from the Coldai Shelter to the saddle above it, from where not only can you see the northwest walls of the Civetta Group, but the majestic 'queen' of the Dolomites — the Marmolada.

One of the best-loved and most beautiful short walks on the Zoldo side of the Civetta Group is the climb up to the Coldai Shelter from the Alleghe Saddle. The chock-a-block parking place at the saddle bears testimony to the popularity of this hike, and you'll also

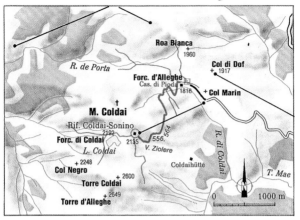

find that the Coldai Shelter is full to overflowing with walkers. Fortunately, not all are staying overnight; more than likely they are day-trippers just enjoying a refreshing drink. There is so much to see around this wonderfully-situated overnight house; you will look out towards Mount Pelmo in the east or the southern Karnish Alps (Cridola, Monfalconi, Duranno, Col Nudo) in the southeast, themselves flanked by the upthrusts of the Bosconero Group to the left and the Prampèr Dolomites on the right.

From the Forcella d'Alleghe to the Coldai Shelter □
Take the well-signposted cart-track (Route 556) and follow its curves up the eastern inclines of Monte Coldai. Later you will bear left on its southeastern corner, to wind your way up through a steep basin to a piece of level ground. From here the way leads westwards to a verdant pause in the mountainside at the uppermost end of the Ziolere Valley, where you will find the shelter.

The descent □ Follow the same route to return.

Opposite: Not far from the Coldai Shelter, walkers enjoy one of the magnificent views in this area — towards Mount Pelmo in the east.

Approach: Listolade (680m/2230ft), a little village at the confluence of the Corpassa and the Cordevole valleys

Starting point/parking: Capanna Trieste (1135m), a bar/ restaurant in the Corpassa Valley, accessible by car via a very poor unsurfaced road from Listolade (4.5km). You can also walk there from Listolade; allow 1h30min.

Overnight suggestion: Vazzolèr Shelter (1714m, run by the Conegliano branch of the Italian Alpine Club, open from 20 June until 20 September, 45 beds, 30 bunks). Refreshments only can be obtained at the Capanna Trieste (1135m, open from 15 July until 15 September).

Walking time: from Capanna Trieste to the Vazzolèr Shelter about 1h30min—1h45min; the return about 1h— 1h15min; *total time between 2h30min—3h*

Grade: a straightforward climb on a mountain road (closed to through traffic)

Highest point: Vazzolèr Shelter (1714m/5620ft), reached after a *climb of 579m/1900ft*

Best time of year: beginning of June until the end of October

---

The mountains around the Vazzolèr Shelter are among the most magnificent in the Dolomites. Make this climb, and you will find yourself suddenly high up opposite sheer towers, escarpments and pinnacles. Yet in the midst of

all this rocky wilderness, you stand in a tranquil oasis, lightly sprinkled with trees. Your 'watering hole', the shelter, is reached via a good road that is closed to traffic, so that you can relax and take in your surroundings. The climb is fairly short and not overly demanding on legs and lungs. . . .

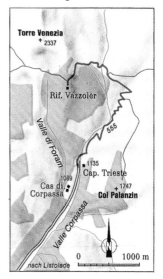

From the Capanna Trieste to the Vazzolèr Shelter □

Follow the motor road (Route 555) into the Corpassa Valley. Before too long you are zig-zagging uphill beneath the Torre Trieste. From around here, there are fabulous views towards the northwest and the Pelsa Ridge, where the Torre Venezia rises to the left. Now continue on steep grassy slopes, heading left (northwest) up towards the Cantoni Valley. Near the end of the climb, having crossed several gulleys, make your way west through a wood of conifers. On reaching a fork, bear left to the shelter.

The descent □ Follow the same route to return.

Opposite: The Torre Venezia stands guard over the Vazzolèr Shelter.

Approach: Agordo (611m/2005ft), a town lying in the basin-like lower Cordevole Valley and an important 'crossroads', or Zoldo (840m/2755ft), an international tourist centre in the Zoldana Valley

Starting point/parking: Passo Duran (1601m). There are two shelters at this pass, the Cesare Tomè and the San Sebastiano. Accessible only by car (14km from Agordo or 14km from Zoldo). Good parking

Overnight suggestions: San Sebastiano Shelter (1600m, private, closed from the end of March until the 20th of June but otherwise always open, 41 beds); or the Carestiato Shelter (1834m, run by the Agordo branch of the Italian Alpine Club, open from 20 June until 20 September, 35 bunks). You can also obtain refreshments at the Cesare Tomè Shelter at the Duran Pass, but there are no facilities for overnight guests.

Walking time: from the Duran Pass to the Carestiato Shelter about 45min–1h; the return about 45min; *total time 1h30min–1h45min*

Grade: a short and easy walk

Highest point: Carestiato Shelter (1834m/6015ft), reached after a *climb of 233m/765ft*

Best time of year: beginning of June until the end of October

---

Set between the Civetta-Moiazza Massif and the Prampèr Dolomites, the Duran Pass is an important gateway between the valleys of Agordo and Zoldo. The fairly recent construction of an overnight shelter at the pass has made it

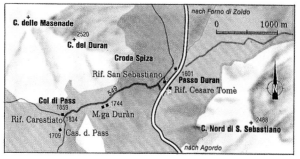

an extremely handy jumping-off point for walkers and climbers. It's also a very good centre for short excursions, like the one described here, which explores the lovely larch-sprinkled uplands southwest of the pass. The rocky area of the Pala Group and the Dolomites around Feltre on the other side of the Cismon Valley make quite a splendid picture — to say nothing of the wonderfully-situated Carestiato shelter, on the southern outcrops of the Moiazza Group. This high-level walk is one which can be undertaken by anyone, and it is highly recommended!

From the Duran Pass to the Carestiato Shelter □ Follow Route 549 (signposted) northwest over larch-covered meadows. You will reach the crossing of an unsurfaced road. Head left (west) along it, through a light wood, going gently up and down, until you come to the meadows around the Casera del Duran (1744m). Continue on the road under the wooded shoulders of the Col dei Pass; it's mostly even going. From here your goal is visible. You have a choice: either follow the road, making a wide arc to the left (west) up to the shelter, or take the more direct route — a path that climbs up through the woods.

The return □ Follow the same route back to the pass.

Opposite: the Carestiato Shelter on the shoulder of the Col dei Pass

Approach: Arabba (1601m/5250ft), a summer resort at the uppermost end of the Cordevole Valley, or Corvara (1555m/5100ft), a health resort in the inner Gader Valley

Starting point/parking: Passo di Campolungo (1875m), a pass between the Sella Group in the west and the Pralongia-Settsass Group in the east. You can get there by car or by bus from Arabba (4km) or Corvara (7km). The exact starting point is the Hotel Boè, some 500m north of the pass, on the Corvara road.

Overnight suggestions: Hotel Boè (1860m, private, open from the beginning of July until the middle of September, 60 beds); or the Pralongia Shelter (2138m, private, open from 20 June until 30 September, 28 beds). You can also obtain refreshments at the Incisa am Incisajoch Restaurant (1935m, private, open year round), but there are no overnight facilities.

Walking time: from the Campolungo Pass to Pralongia about 1h30min; the return about 1h—1h15min; *total time between 2h30min—2h45min*

Grade: an easy walk

Highest point: Pralongia (2138m/7010ft), reached after a *climb of 263m/860ft*

Best time of year: mid-June until the end of October

The famed winter skiing area around the Pralongia summit has a lot to offer the summer visitor — so long as you keep clear of the closed-off areas around the lifts. One delightful — and little-frequented — walk is described

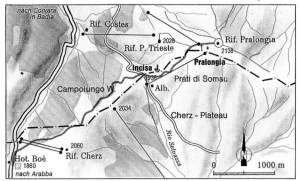

here. It follows part of the Dolomite 'High-Level Route' 9 and travels from the Campo-lungo Pass to the shelter on the sub-alpine summit of Pralongia. Walking within sight of the Sella and Puez Groups, we go over meadow-land up to the Incisajoch, a saddle from where there is a splendid view of the Civetta. When we come to the end of the walk, not only is there a well-run shelter, but a panorama towards the mountains in the area of the Abtei and Cordevole valleys.

From the Campolungo Pass to the Pralongia Shelter □

Take the road from the Hotel Boè and head along in the direction of Corvara for about 300m (yards) downhill. Then turn right onto Route 3, a footpath waymarked with red paint. You climb the western flanks of the Cherz Plateau; most of the time you're in a fir wood (lots of bilberries!). Climbing gently, you finally bear right in a broad pastureland basin and go through it, heading east, to the Incisajoch, a saddle between Mount Cherz in the south and Pralongia in the northeast. From here take the steep track over treeless pastureland, to curve north to a mountainside shoulder. The track bears right here and climbs steeply to the peak.

The return □ Follow the same route back.

Opposite: a little chapel on the track to Pralongia

Approach: Agordo (611m/2005ft), a town lying in the basin-like lower Cordevole Valley and an important 'crossroads'

Starting point/parking: Col di Prà (843m), a hamlet at the upper end of the San Lucano Valley. There are two restaurants here: Al Cacciatori (private, open from 10 June to 31 August, 2 beds) and Col di Prà (private, open from 10 June to 31 August, 8 beds). Col di Prà is accessible by car only (10km from Agordo).

Overnight suggestion: Dordei Shelter ('Bivacco Dordei', 1309m, run by the Italian Alpine Club Trieste, always open — but not always under supervision, 9 bunks)

Walking time: from Col di Prà to the Angheraz Valley and on to the shelter about 1h30min—2h; the return about 1h; *total time about 2h30min—3h*

Grade: a climb on well-signposted tracks and paths

Highest point: Dordei Shelter (1309m/4295ft), reached after a *climb of 466m/1530ft*

Best time of year: beginning of June until the end of October

San Lucano's valley, which branches off from the Cordevole Valley at Taibon Agordino, is one of the least-visited areas in the central Pala Massif. The best way to get to this ravine, where the rock walls seem to penetrate the heavens, is by car via the little hamlet of Col di Prà. From here you will look up with astonishment at the gigantic four-sided tower of the

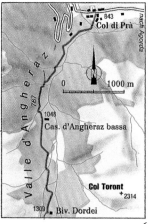

Mount Agnèr peak, with its 1500m-high north wall. It's one of the major showplaces of the Dolomites! Of the many excursions you can make in this area, one of the best is a visit to the Angheraz Valley, set between the central Pala Group in the west and the lonely heights of the southern Pala Group in the

Monte Agnèr from the northwest, seen from the San Lucano Valley

east. Once in the Angheraz, you can climb up the canyon-like continuation of the Lucano Valley to the Dordei Shelter. Hardly anyone ever comes this way, although other routes in the Pala mountains are very popular.

From Col di Prà through the Angheraz Valley to the Dordei Shelter □

A forestry road closed to through traffic heads west from Col di Prà. Don't continue on it; instead bear left on Route 767 (signposted), to follow the Torrente Tegnas south. It's quite a steep climb through woods to the pasturelands, where the valley flattens out at the Casera d'Angheraz. From here the signposted path heads south (sometimes in a dry streambed) up to the shelter. It rests below the mighty massif of the Croda Grande, Coro and Alberghetto peaks.

The return □ Follow the same route to descend.

Approach: San Martino di Castrozza (1466m/4810ft), a summer and winter sports centre in the Cismon Valley, or Predazzo (1018m/3340ft), a market village at the confluence of the Tavignolo and Fleims valleys

Parking/funicular: Rolle Pass (1980m), between the Fleimstal Alps in the west and the Pala Group in the east. This is accessible by car or bus from San Martino (10km) or Predazzo (21km). Take the chair lift from the pass (located a bit downhill to the east) to the Segantini Bar.

Starting point: Segantini Bar (Bàita; 2174m), above the Rolle Pass to the east, between the Rolle and Costazza peaks

Overnight suggestion: none, but you can obtain refreshments at the Segantini Bar (private, open all year round)

Walking time: from the Segantini Bar back downhill to the Rolle Pass *30min total time*

Grade: easy — on a road or good paths

Highest point: Segantini Bar (2174m/7130ft), from where there is a *descent of 202m/660ft*

Best time of year: mid-June until mid-October

Hint: It's worth the effort to climb to either the Costazza or Rolle peaks, once you're up at the Segantini Bar; there are wonderful views.

The bold obelisk of the Cimon della Pala — which is reminiscent of the Matterhorn — and the smooth-sided trapezoid of the Vezzana Peak are among the striking views you'll have from the Rolle Pass. But even more splendid is the perspective you have of the towering rock

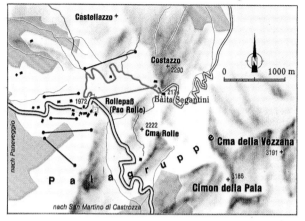

of the Pala once you're up at the Bàita (Bar) Segantini! You can easily reach this viewpoint, shown opposite, by taking the chair lift up from the Rolle Pass. Then enjoy the easy walk back down: either follow the road, or else shorten the descent by taking a footpath. When you're at the log cabin-like shelter, you'll be just below the gigantic pillars and walls of the Vezzana-Cimon Massif — it's a landscape not only full of harmony, but one of great majesty as well.

Descent from the Segantini Bar to the pass □
From the shelter follow the unsurfaced road west under the chairlift, then curve down over the green slopes to the chair lift station and back to the pass along the asphalt road.

Note: On the descent, if you like, you can take a footpath: it heads off left from the unsurfaced road just where you pass under the chair lift. This goes off in a westerly direction over pasture-lands and ends up back at the top of the chair lift.

Opposite: The bold obelisk of the Cimon della Pala rises just above you when you visit the Segantini Bar, a cabin-like building on the slopes above the Rolle Pass.

Approach: Fiera di Primiero (713m/2340ft), an important market centre on the northern edge of the Primör Basin

Starting point/parking: Cant del Gal (1160m), at the confluence of the Pradidali and Canali valleys, accessible by car (8km from Fiera di Primiero)

Overnight suggestions: Albergo-Ristorante Cant del Gal (1160m, private, open from the beginning of June until the end of October, 18 beds); or the Treviso Shelter (1631m, run by the Treviso branch of the Italian Alpine Club, open from 1 June until 5 October, 36 beds)

Walking time: from Cant del Gal to the Treviso Shelter about 1h30min; the return about 1h; *total time 2h30min*

Grade: a straightforward climb on a good unsurfaced road and wide trail

Highest point: Treviso Shelter (1631m/5350ft), reached after a *climb of 471m/1545ft*

Best time of year: beginning of June until the end of October

Hint: You could also walk from Cant del Gal to the lovely larch-studded meadows of Piereni, from where you would have wonderful views of the peaks surrounding the inner Canali Valley (see photograph). Approach Piereni (and its guesthouse) either on foot or by car, by following the unsurfaced road heading southwest towards the Col di Cistri.

Pale, mighty, unapproachable — these words sum up the mountains at the heart of the Canali Valley. This impressive divide is flanked on the north by the grand central massif of the

Pala and on the south by the majestic row of towers crowning the little-known southern Pala Group. But even if you do not penetrate into the higher rocky regions, this landscape will make a strong impression on you and stay in your memory for a very long time.

From Cant del Gal through the inner Canali Valley and to the Treviso Shelter □

Take the unsurfaced road (Route 707, 711) on the left-hand side of the inner valley and head northeast through a light forest. We climb to a barrier (where there is a small car park) and then on a relatively even contour to the end of the motorable road. Here Route 711 turns left (signposted). We cross the dry streambed of the Canali and continue up the right-hand side of the stream (Route 707), heading northeast through a wood. The crossing of the Dolomite 'High-Level Route' 2 is met (signposted). From here the path zig-zags steeply up the wooded slope to the right (east), and we reach the shelter.

The return □ The descent follows the same route.

Opposite: in the lower Canali Valley

Approach: Fiera di Primero (713m/2340), an important market centre on the northern edge of the Primör Basin, or Agordo (611m/2005ft), a town lying in the basin-like lower Cordevole Valley and an important 'crossroads'

Starting point/parking: Passo Cereda (1361m), a pass between the Pala Group in the north and the mountains around Feltre in the south. The pass is accessible by car or by bus from Fiera di Primiero (9km) or Agordo (24km).

Overnight suggestion: Passo Cereda Shelter (1361m, private, open all year round, 35 beds). You can also obtain refreshments at the Malga Fossetta, a dairy farm (1556m, private, open in the summer only).

Walking time: from the Passo Cereda to the Passo Palughet about 1h15min; the return about 45min; total time *2h*

Grade: well-signposted forestry roads and footpaths; however, the climb is quite steep in places

Highest point: Palughet Pass (1910m/6265ft), reached after a *climb of 549m/1800ft*

Best time of year: mid-June until the end of October

Hint: If you like, you can drive up a narrow forestry road to the dairy (Malga Fossetta), saving 45 minutes.

'C imonega' — get to know this mountain landscape on the southwest side of the Dolomites! These towering peaks lie between the Cismon, Mis and Piave valleys. The gigantic

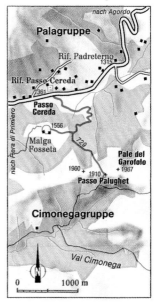

Sass de Mura and the cyclopean wedge of the Piz de Sagron are just sensational! If you want to find yourself standing just opposite these giants, marvelling at even more bright jewels in this Dolomite setting, then climb up from the Cedera Pass to the dairy at Malga Fossetta and go on to the Palughet Pass. If you're lucky enough to be here when the evening sun casts its shadows, you will see an unbelievably beautiful panorama.

From the Cereda Pass to the Palughet Pass via the Malga Fossetta □
Follow the unsurfaced road south; it curves up to a pastureland-saddle and the Malga Fossetta, a dairy-farm from where there are very good views. At the start of the meadows, you lose the road: walk south (left) to a water tank. Here go left on Route 729, following the verdant northern slopes of the mountain. The route curves, but heads generally east up to the scree line on the north side of the Palughet Pass. First cross a short section of scree, then go over the grassy strip on its left and finally up to the pass.

The return □ The descent follows the same route.

Opposite: the Cimonega Group, seen from the north

Approach: Mezzano (640m/2100ft), located in the middle of the Primör Basin

Starting point/parking: Mezzano (good parking)

Overnight suggestion: The Caltena Shelter (1265m, private, open from 1 June until 30 September, 8 beds, 4 bunks)

Walking time: from Mezzano to the Caltena Shelter (ascent) about 1h30min; from the Caltena Shelter to Fiera di Primiero (descent) about 45min; *total time about 2h15min*

Grade: a straightforward climb on well-signposted cart-tracks or roads

Highest point: Caltena Shelter (1265m/4150ft), reached after a *climb of 625m/2050ft*

Best time of year: from Easter until the beginning of November

---

*T*he larch-graced meadows of Caltena are indescribably beautiful. Walks around this gem of an alpine setting — halfway up the mountains — are always enchanting, set as they are against a backdrop of the Pala towers and the summits of the Sass de Mura and the Piz di Sagron in the Cimonega Group. A wonderful circular hike is described here: it takes us from Mezzano to Rines and Poit, then up to the Caltena Shelter. From there we follow an unsurfaced road down to Fiera di Primiero. Here we can catch a bus back to Mezzano.

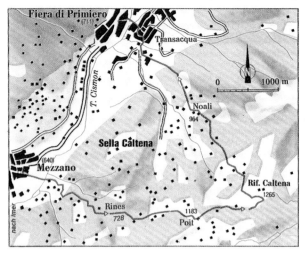

Climb from Mezzano to the Caltena Shelter □

Follow the road out of Mezzano that crosses the Cismon *torrente*; you will come to the hamlet of Coppera. From there continue on a cart-track (Route 728) to the pasturelands of Rines (see opposite). Cross the meadows, heading uphill through woods to the crossing of the Caltena meadow-basin, which is reached when you get to a fork at the hamlet of Poit (there is a crucifix here). Head left (northeast) to follow the basin on a motorable road. You make your way gently uphill to the Caltena Shelter.

Descent from the Caltena Shelter to Fiera di Primiero □

Head westwards along the unsurfaced road to the wayside shrine dedicated to Saint Anthony. From here, first cross the wonderful larch-covered meadows of Sicone, winding downhill; then continue downhill through woods, heading northwest, to the hamlet of Noali. From here it's a fairly steep descent down a gulley to Transaqua on the outskirts of Fiera di Primiero. In Fiera itself, you can get a bus back to Mezzano.

Opposite: looking towards the Pala Group from Rines

Approach: Imèr (645m/2115ft), an international tourist centre at the southern end of the Primör Basin, opposite the confluence of the Noana and Cismon valleys

Starting point/parking: Imèr

Overnight suggestion: Fonteghi Shelter (1100m, private, open from 15 June until 30 September, 9 beds)

Walking time: from Imèr to the Fonteghi Shelter via Val Noana about 1h45min–2h; from the shelter back to Imèr via Valpiana di Sopra and Val Noana about 1h 45min–2h; *total time between 3h30min–4h*

Grade: a straightforward walk on well-signposted roads and cart-tracks; moderate climb

Highest point: Valpiana di Sopra (1166m/3825ft), reached after a *climb of 521m/1710ft*

Best time of year: beginning of May until mid-November, but at its most beautiful in early spring (when the snow is melting) or in autumn (when the leaves are changing colour)

One of the loveliest areas in the Dolomites around Feltre is the confluence of the Val Noana and the Val Cismon. Do try to see it when the snow is melting in early spring and waterfalls pour off the walls of the Noana Gorge. It's also a wonderful experience in summertime, after a day of heavy summer showers. The walk leads up the Noana Gorge to the picturesque Noana Reservoir and then to the idyllic Fonteghi Shelter, before finally reaching the broad pastureland saddle called 'Valpiana di Sopra'. Here you will be just below the peaks

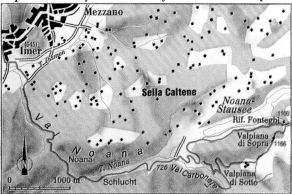

From Valpiana di Sopra you look out towards Monte Pavione — the most beautiful grassy peak in the Alps.

of the Feltre Range. Above them all, Monte Pavione stands out: it's know as the 'most beautiful pyramid of grass in the Alps'.

From Imèr to the Fonteghi Shelter via the Noana Gorge □

Follow the unsurfaced road southeast, to cross the Cismon and come to the foot of the Sella Caltena. Here, first go right, then sharp left into the Noana Gorge, flanked by high rock walls. Now just follow the road (Route 726) up to the widening of the gorge where it is joined by the Carbonere Valley. This latter valley is then followed by curving steeply uphill, until a fork is reached. Here turn left, back into the Val Noana. On coming to a wooded ridge (from where Lake Noana is already visible), bear right to continue on even ground. You'll pass through a forest and then reach the Fonteghi Shelter.

From the Fonteghi Shelter to Imèr via Valpiana and the Noana Gorge □

On the right-hand side of the pastureland, head south up to the hamlet of Valpiana di Sopra, where you will cross a saddle and then bear right downhill to Valpiana di Sotto ('Lower Valpiana'). From here follow the meadows to the west, go through a wood and come to the crossing of an unsurfaced road. Bear right on the road; it will take you down to the Noana road, which you then descend back to Imèr.

Approach: Feltre (324m/1060ft), a lovely city in the Piave Valley with many artistic monuments; also an important 'crossroads'

Starting point/parking: Albergo Alpino (660m), in the upper Canzoi Valley below the walls of the Lago della Stua. Accessible by car from Feltre (via Soranzen, 18km)

Overnight suggestion: The Alpino Inn (660m, private, open all year round, 22 beds)

Walking time: from the Alpino Inn to the southern ridge of the Punta di Comedon about 1h45min—2h; the return about 1h15min; *total time 3h—3h15min*

Grade: Sure-footedness is essential! Up to the fork in the Caorame Valley the footpath is well-signposted, but beyond there the waymarking is haphazard, and the footpaths hard to follow and potentially dangerous. Only experienced mountain walkers should attempt this part of the hike. Otherwise, return to the inn from the fork.

Highest point: southern ridge of the Punta di Comedon (about 1180m/3870ft), reached after a *climb of 520m/ 1705ft*

Best time of year: May to November

Canzoi's Valley is one of the least-visited in all the Dolomites. Here you will see the mighty peaks of the Cimonega, Brandol, Tre Pietre and Feltre Range rising high and lonely. This is a mountain world that has not yet come under the aegis of the 'Dolomites National Park'

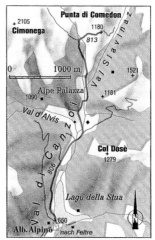

and remains 'under-developed' — thank goodness. From the Alpino Inn you can take a track into the upper part of the valley and climb from there to a superb viewing point on the south side of the Punta di Comedon, from where there is a wonderful panorama over the wild and luxuriant heart of the Canzoi Valley.

From the Alpino Inn through the upper Canzoi Valley to the viewpoint (Punta di Comedon) □

Follow the unsurfaced road, winding up north to the Lago della Stua. Then follow its left bank up into the valley. You'll climb gently through a wood and come to the end of the road. Here take Route 806, signposted for 'Biv. Feltre-Walter Bodo'. This footpath follows the left-hand side of the Caorame Valley and zig-zags up through a forest of deciduous trees. The stream is crossed, and we continue to zig-zag up the right-hand side of the valley to a wall and a fork. From here on, the waymarking is poor and the path potentially dangerous. Follow Route 813 to the east along the very steep inclines, crossing several ridges. There is no definite 'end' to this walk, but when you are at an altitude of about 1180m, you should find views like the one shown opposite, where the entire upper valley lies at your feet.

The descent □ Follow the same route to return.

Opposite: the upper Canzoi Valley, seen from a pause on the southern flanks of the Punta di Comedon

Approach: Fiera di Primiero (713m/2340ft), an important market centre on the northern edge of the Primör Basin, or Agordo (611m/2005ft), a town lying in the basin-like lower Cordevole Valley and an important 'crossroads'

Starting point/parking: Passo Cereda (1361m), a pass between the Pala Group in the north and the mountains around Feltre in the south. The pass is accessible by car or by bus from Fiera di Primiero (9km) or Agordo (24km).

Overnight suggestions: Passo Cereda Shelter (1361m, private, open all year round, 35 beds); or the hotel in Sagron. You can also obtain refreshments at the Padreterno Shelter (1316m).

Walking time: from the Cereda Pass to Sagron about 1h–1h15min; the return about 1h15min–1h30min; *total time between 2h15min–2h45min*

Grade: a straightforward climb on an unsurfaced road (closed to traffic)

Highest point: Cereda Pass, from where there is a descent to Sagron. On the return, you have a *climb of 299m/ 980ft*

Best time of year: possible all year round, but at its best in early summer or on clear autumn days

T he Cereda Pass, situated between the Pala Group and the mountains around Feltre, is the hub of some very good short walks in the area. Two of the best are the hike described in Walk 31 (to the Palughet Pass) and the walk described here, which visits Sagron, a village set on the northeastern slopes of the

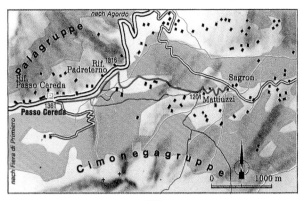

Sagron, with the Tàmer Group in the background

Cimonega Group, high above the Mis Valley. This tiny village, with its church perched on a hilltop and its far-reaching views to the mountains around Belluno and Agordo, is easily reached by car. But it's far more fun to walk along the unsurfaced road that goes there from the Cereda Pass via the little hamlet of Mattiuzzi. This unsurfaced road is closed to traffic and forms part of the Dolomite 'High-Level Route' 2.

From the Cereda Pass to Sagron via Mattiuzzi □ Walk east along the asphalt Cereda Pass road, heading towards Agordo. About 1.5km downhill you'll come to the Padreterno Shelter (where you can get some refreshments). Beyond here, continue on the asphalt road for just a little longer, then turn right onto the unsurfaced road on the north side of the Cimonega Group. Head east through forest and over meadows, on even ground, until you come to a fork. A right turn would take you into the hamlet of Mattiuzzi; the main walk goes straight ahead through pastureland and curves downhill to Sagron. There are very fine views along the way.

The return □ The return walk follows the same route, and you climb back up to the Cereda Pass.

Approach: Wolkenstein (1566m/5135ft), a health resort in the upper Gröden Valley, or Canazei (1450m/4755ft), at the end of the Fassa Valley

Starting point/parking: Sellajoch (2213m), a saddle between the Sella and Langkofel groups, accessible by car or bus from Wolkenstein (9km) or Canazei (12km). The exact starting point is the Great Dolomite Road below the saddle.

Overnight suggestions: Sellajochhaus (2183m, run by the Bozen branch of the Italian Alpine Club, open from the beginning of June until the end of October, 52 beds, 14 bunks); the Grohman Shelter (2222m, private, open from the beginning of July until 15 September, 14 beds); Friedrich-August Shelter (2298m, private, open from mid-June until mid-October, 16 beds, 15 bunks); or the Plattkofel Shelter (2301m, private, open from 20 June until 10 October, 37 beds)

Walking time: from the Sellajoch to the Fassajoch about 1h30min–2h; the return about 1h30min–2h; *total time 3–4h*

Grade: a very easy high-level walk

Highest point: Forcella Col Rodella, a saddle at 2318m/7605ft, reached after a *climb of 105m/345ft*

Best time of year: mid-June until mid-October

Friedrich-August-Weg and Bindelweg (Walk 37) are high-level walks in the realm of that 'queen' of the Dolomites, the Marmolada. Both walks are similar, but not identical, in character. Whereas dark volcanic stone characterises the Bindelweg, on this walk we wander through a

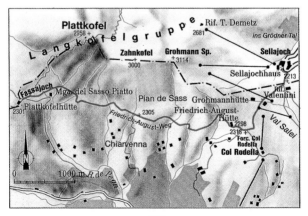

The Langkofel Massif, with the Grohmanspitze and the Fünffinger- ('Five-fingered'-) Spitze

landscape of mighty golden-red dolomitic rock, which makes a wonderful contrast with the glistening, snow-covered inclines of the Marmolada. Do allow an entire day for this walk, so that you can do the return Fassajoch—Sellajoch in the afternoon, when the pristine white beauty of the Marmolada will be spotlighted for you!

From the Sellajoch to the Fassajoch via the Friedrich-August-Weg □
Follow the asphalt road from the Sellajochhaus uphill for a short way, then turn right on a track (Route 4) to cross the actual saddle and descend to the Valentini Shelter below left. Continue along the grassy eastern slopes of the Langkofel Massif to the Grohmann Shelter and from there head south. Eventually you climb in wide loops up to a saddle, the Forcella Col Rosella. Here the route turns to the south side of the Langkofel Group, and we descend to the Friedrich August Shelter. Finally, the high-level walk takes us west along green slopes to the Fassajoch and welcome refreshments at the Plattkofel 'Hut'.

The return □ Follow the same route back, preferably in the afternoon.

Approach: Canazei (1450m/4755ft); see Walk 36.

Parking/funicular: Park at the Pecol cabin lift station in Canazei and take the cabin lift up to Pecol (1926m), from where you continue by chair lift to the Sasso Becce Shelter (2423m).

Starting point: Sasso Becce Shelter (2423m)

Overnight suggestions: Sasso Becce Shelter (2423m, private, open from 1 July until 10 September, 10 beds); Vial del Pan Shelter (2432m, private, open from 20 May until 20 October, 15 bunks); or the E Castiglioni Shelter (2044m, run by the Milan branch of the Italian Alpine Club, open year round, 50 beds, 30 bunks). You can also obtain refreshments at the Bar Fredarola (summer only).

Walking time: from the Sasso Becce Shelter to the Fedaia Pass, *total walking time about 2h–2h30min*

Grade: an easy high-level walk

Highest point: Vial del Pan Shelter (2432m/7980ft), from where there is a *descent of 388m/1275ft*

Best time of year: beginning of July until the end of September

---

Bindelweg, described here, and Friedrich-August-Weg (Walk 36) are two of the most famous and spectacular walks in the Dolomites. Why these in particular? Possibly because these routes do not cross 'typical' Dolomite landscapes; they both lie in the confines of the Marmolada Massif. This range, when seen from the north, is far more reminiscent of the central Alps because of its large glacial formations.

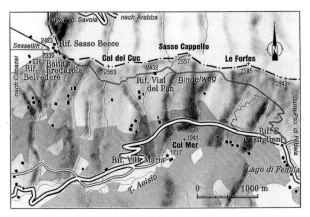

Looking towards the peaks of the Langkofel and Sella groups from the Bindelweg

Another reason for the popularity of this ramble might be the contrasts between the 'queen' — Marmolada — and her entourage, which are fascinating when seen from this vantage point. Whatever the reason, thanks to the lifts and the good bus connections, you can do this walk easily as a day's outing from Canazei. From the top of the chair lift, you amble around the green southern slopes of the dark volcanic Padon Group; all along the way, you're accompanied by views over to the glistening glaciers of Marmolada.

From the Sasso Becce Shelter to the Passo Fedaia via the Bindelweg □
From the chair lift, walk east to a saddle and the Bar Fredarola. From here take the well-marked path (Route 601), to make a large arc around the grassy flanks of Col del Cuc and Sasso Cappello. At first the way is even; then a very short ascent takes you to the Vial del Pan Shelter on the south side of Sasso Cappello. Carry on to a gap on the east side of the mountain, then head east in the large pastureland basin under the lookout point. From here the route descends the steep, craggy inclines — first by heading to the right — down to the Passo Fedaia.

The return □
Take a bus from the pass to Canazei.

Approach: Pozza di Fassa (1310m/4295ft), a summer resort at the confluence of the San Nicolo and Fassa valleys

Starting point/parking: Bàita Campiè (1826m), halfway up the San Nicolo Valley (7km from Pozzo by car)

Overnight suggestion: none, but between 1 July and 25 September you can get refreshments at the Bar Campiè

Walking time: Bar Campiè to the lake (Lagusèl) about 45min–1h; return about 30min; *total time 1h30min*

Grade: undemanding and well-signposted walk

Highest point: Lagusèl (2103m/6895ft), reached after a *climb of 277m/910ft*

Best time of year: end of June until the beginning of November

Hints: From the lake at the end of this walk, you can climb for 15 minutes up south to the Pief, a saddle from where there are wonderful views down into the Monzoni Valley to the west. Reach the saddle by turning right (west), when you come to Route 641. There is also the possibility of following Route 641 to the east (left): this would take you back to the Bar Campiè via the Forcetta Pecol, a saddle at 2259m (reckon on 1h30min).

---

*S*urprisingly, there are some areas in the Alps that are very little frequented — even though they have excellent footpaths and are well documented in the guidebooks. Perhaps

it is because they are lacking in the really dramatic mountain scenery that always attracts walkers and photographers. Whatever the reason, they remain undervalued and 'unloved'. One of these areas is the western part of the Marmolada Group, in particular the mountain landscape between the Fassa and Pellegrino valleys. We explore this setting — in particular the area

around the San Nicolo and Monzoni valleys, where a tiny jewel of a lake lies hidden in a basin on the slopes of Mount Palon.

From the Bar Campiè to the lake (Lagusèl) □
A signpost at the bar points our way to a footpath waymarked in red (no route number). First we cross the Rio San Nicolo and then continue in a westerly direction through a lovely forest of conifers to the joining of Route 640 (on our right). We follow this southwest, winding up in large curves to climb over a steep wooded ridge. After crossing a stream, we head right and continue climbing (though less steeply) through magnificent conifers up to a treeless meadow where there are scattered huts. Go straight past a beautiful crucifix and very gently upwards past the Pièf Saddle to the lake. 'Lagusèl' is set like a gem: it lies in a basin between the peaks of Palon to the west and Pecol to the east.

The descent □ Follow the same route to return.

Opposite: Lagusèl, a gem-like lake in the Marmoladas

Approach: Kaltern (426m/1395ft), a well-known wine district southwest of Bozen (Bolzano), set on the banks of the Überetsch

Parking/funicular: Park at the station for the Mendel cable car in St Anton (523m), 16km from Bozen. You can also get here by bus from Bozen. Take the cable car up to the Mendel Pass.

Starting point: Mendel Pass (1363m)

Overnight suggestions: There are various hotels and guest-houses at the Mendel Pass; also the Roènalm (1773m, private, open from 1 June until 15 October, 15 bunks). You can obtain refreshments only at the Enzian Shelter (1421m, open all year round) and the Halbweg Hütte ('Halfway Hut', 1595m, open all year round).

Walking time: from the Mendel Pass to Mount Roèn about 2h45min–3h; return about 2h; *total time under 5h*

Grade: a straightforward, but quite long walk, with a noticeable climb

Highest point: Mount Roèn (2116m/6940ft), reached after a *climb of 753m/2470ft*

Best time of year: mid-June until mid-October

Hint: From the Roènalm you can take a very enjoyable walk (30min) to a shelter high above the Etsch Valley, following the eastern inclines of Mount Roèn.

---

*I*f you like walking under tall firs, listening to the whispers in the treetops, then the climb up Mount Roèn is just the walk for you. You set out from the Mendel Pass, easily reached by cable car from Kaltern. Here a high mountain trail

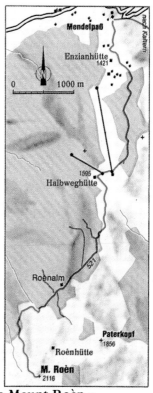

takes you through a forest of proud fir trees to the Roèn pasturelands and then to the peak. When you leave the cover of the forest, the views open out to reveal panoramic views encompassing a good part of the southern Alps. But your most lasting memory of this walk may well be the fascinating views down into the Etsch Valley, for you will look straight down onto the grape-growing centre of Tramin, no less than 1800m — 5905ft below!

From the Mendel Pass to Mount Roèn □
From the cable car station walk past the Schönblick Guesthouse. Just beyond it, take the cement path heading left. It takes you to an unsurfaced road (Route 521). Follow the road left (south) up along the wooded ridge, and you will come to the Enzian Shelter. At the fork, go straight ahead and through woods to a flat pastureland studded with larch trees. Soon you're back in the forest and on a track; it climbs to the 'Halfway' Shelter. Keep up the wooded ridge to reach a grassy saddle and the Roénalm (where there is also a shelter). From here the way climbs steeply to the right, rounding the western side of the mountain to attain the peak.

Descent □ Follow the same route to return.

Opposite: the view from the Mendel Pass

Approach: Andalo (1041m/3415ft), on the broad pastureland saddle between the central Brenta and the lower Paganella groups, or Molveno (868m/2850ft), a summer resort beside the lake of the same name, on the eastern side of the Brenta Group

Parking/funicular: Park at the station for the Paganella cabin lift in Andalo. Travel with the lift up to the peak of Paganella.

Starting point: Paganella Shelter (2098m), at the upper end of the cabin lift

Overnight suggestion: Cesare Battisti Shelter (2098m, run by the Italian Alpine Club SAT Trento, open all year round, 23 beds). You can also obtain refreshments at the Paganella Shelter (2108m, private), but there are no overnight facilities.

Walking time: from Paganella to Molveno, *total time 2h—2h30min.* Return by bus or taxi from Molveno to Andalo.

Grade: a long descent on a well-signposted track; *total descent 1319m/4325ft*

Best time of year: beginning of June until the beginning of October

---

Try to do this walk in the autumn, when the valleys are so full of thick mist that you can't see down into them. Then, when you get up to the Paganella peak and shelter, you'll find yourself high above the Etschtal, lost to the world below, on a 'blissful island' all your own. In the west, the Brenta Group will be fully visible. . . . If, however, you come on a

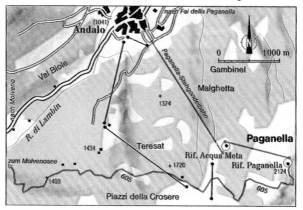

clear day, the views will be magnificent, and you might even catch the mirror-reflections of Lake Garda to the far south! Of the three lifts to the top of Paganella, we take the one climbing the northwest side. From the top, it's all downhill and such an easy walk that you can take the children along, too.

The descent from Paganella to Molveno □
From the Paganella Shelter at the top end of the cabin lift, follow Route 605 west over pasture-land and through dwarf pines. You come to a hut at Malga Terlago (1826m), from where you pick up Route 605. First the way passes over treeless terrain, but later you will be descending through woodlands as you sweep down to Lake Molveno. Here pick up the San Lorenzo in Banale–Molveno road. Follow it to the west and curve up to Molveno. From here you can get a bus back to Andalo.

Opposite: the Brenta Group

Approach: Molveno (864m/2835ft), a summer resort beside the lake of the same name, on the eastern side of of the Brenta Group

Parking/funicular: Park in Molveno. Take the chair lift to Pradèl at 1365m — it's the middle station on the lift.

Starting point: Pradèl (1365m), a large pastureland shoulder above Molveno

Overnight suggestions: Pradèl Shelter (1365m, private, open from 1 June until 30 September, 40 beds); Pradèl Inn and Restaurant (1365m, private, open from 1 June until 30 September, 36 beds); Croz dell'Altissimo Shelter (1450m, private, open from 20 June until 20 September, 6 beds); or Selvata Shelter (1630m, private, open from 20 June until 20 September, 16 beds)

Walking time: from Pradèl to the Selvata Shelter (ascent) about 1h15min—1h45min; from the Selvata Shelter to Molveno via the Valle delle Seghe (descent) about 1h 30min; *total time between 2h45min—3h15min*

Grade: an easy circular walk; well signposted

Highest point: Selvata Shelter (1630m/5345ft), reached after a *climb of 263m/860ft*

Best time of year: mid-June until the end of September

In contrast with the much-frequented footpaths on the west side of the Brenta Group, those in the east are much less visited, due to the steep gradients to be mastered. The route this walk follows is hardly ever visited either (even though

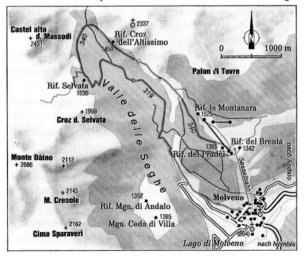

Cime Brenta and the Tuckett Pass, seen from the Valle delle Seghe

it's very easy). You will enjoy wonderful views to the central massif of the Brenta Group. Then, if you make the short climb to the west over the Selvata Shelter, you can also admire the mighty Croz dell'Altissimo on the other side of the valley.

From Pradèl to the Selvata Shelter via the Croz dell'Altissimo Shelter □

Take the level cart-track (Route 340) on the right-hand edge of the Seghe Valley and head northwest, first going through woods and scrub. Later you pass under the massive southwest wall of the Croz dell'Altissimo and reach the shelter up in the valley (1450m). Now make a leftward arc, crossing a band of scree, and going over to the other side of the valley, from where the route winds up to the Selvata Shelter.

Return through the Seghe Valley to Molveno □

Go back a short way along Route 340, then head right on Route 319 (the turn-off is sign-posted). Zig-zag down through woods to the floor of the Valle delle Seghe. Here take the track (Route 319) to head southeast out of the valley and on to Molveno.

Approach: Madonna di Campiglio (1514m/4965ft), a well-known international tourist centre on the west side of the Brenta Group

Starting point/parking: Vallesinella Shelter (1513m), in an offshoot of the Brenta Valley southeast from Madonna di Campiglio, accessible by car via an unsurfaced road (5km)

Overnight suggestions: Vallesinella Shelter (1513m, private, open from 20 June until 20 September, 30 beds); Casinei Shelter (1825m, private, open from 15 June until 10 October, 28 beds); or Brentei Shelter (2182m, run by the Monza branch of the Italian Alpine Club, open from 20 June until 20 September, 80 beds)

Walking time: from the Vallesinella Shelter to the Brentei Shelter about 2h; the return about 1h–1h15min; *total time under 3h15min*

Grade: a straightforward, but strenuous, climb

Highest point: Brentei Shelter (2182m/7155ft), reached after a *climb of 669m/2195ft*

Best time of year: beginning of June until mid-October

---

*I*f you would like to see a mountain landscape translated from a theatrical backdrop into reality, you'll find it here in the Brenta! The price to be paid is a steep, but uncomplicated, climb high up over the Brenta Valley to the Brentei Shelter along the 'Bogani Footpath'. En route you will be accompanied by far-reaching views to the glaciers of the Adamello and Presanella groups. Then, suddenly, the gigantic rock obelisk of the Crozzon di Brenta, with its 1000m-high northern slope, comes into

Along the Bogani Footpath ('Sentiero Bogani')

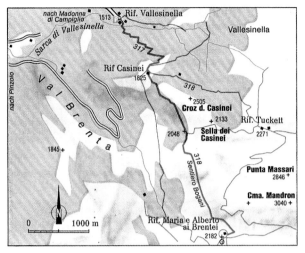

view. Finally you come to the basin of the Val Brenta Alta, where the unforgettable Brentei Shelter lies surrounded by bizarre towers and giant rock walls.

From the Vallesinella Shelter to the Brentei Shelter via the 'Sentiero Bogani' □
Take Route 317 from the Vallesinella Shelter and cross a wooded slope, zig-zagging up southeast to the Casinei Shelter, located on a mountainside shoulder from where there are very fine views. From here follow Route 318 (the 'Bogani Footpath'). It takes you high up over the Brenta Valley, first through woods and then over treeless terrain on the western flanks of the Cima Brenta Massif. On reaching a fork, where Route 322 goes left, continue straight ahead to a mountain shelf from where there is an especially good view of the Crozzon. Now continue on the widening trail through perpendicular walls and into a short tunnel. On the other side, a noticeable rocky upthrust is approached (on your right). From here cross a flat basin to the south, and you will come to the Brentei Shelter.

The return □ Follow the same route to descend.

Approach: Madonna di Campiglio (1514m/4965ft), a well-known international tourist centre on the west side of the Brenta Group

Parking/funicular: Park in Madonna di Campiglio at the station for the Funivia 5 Laghi ('Five-Lake-Funicular'). Take the cabin lift up to the Pancùgolo Shelter.

Starting point: Pancùgolo Shelter (2064m), near the top of the cabin lift on Mount Palon

Overnight suggestion: none, but you can obtain refreshments at the Pancùgolo Shelter (2064m, open year-round) or the Ristorante Malga Ritorto (1747m).

Walking time: from the Pancùgolo Shelter to Lake Ritorto 15min; from the lake back to Madonna di Campiglio (descent) about 2h15min; *total time 2h30min*

Grade: an easy descent on well-signposted tracks and forestry roads

Highest point: Pancùgolo Shelter (2064m/6770ft), from where there is a *descent of 550m/1805ft*

Best time of year: beginning of June until the end of September

---

*T*he many mountain lakes on the eastern flanks of the Presanella Group are like gems sparkling in their severe setting — a granite landscape hewn and polished by Ice Age glaciers. The finest jewel in the collection is undoubtedly Lake Ritorto, easily reached by lift from Madonna di Campiglio. The mighty rock formations of the Brenta Group are reflected in its crystal-clear waters; their mirror-image is unforgettably beautiful. From here you can enjoy a

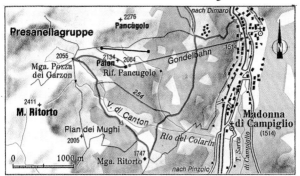

gentle walk down into the Campiglio Valley. Try to make this descent through lovely woodlands and across wide meadows in the early evening, when the Brenta escarpment is reddened by the setting sun.

From the Pancùgolo Shelter to Lake Ritorto □ Take the wide trail (Route 232; some of it has been blasted from the rock) along the steep southern flanks of the Palon, heading west. It's level walking to the lake, set in a circular basin.

Descent from Lake Ritorto to Madonna di Campiglio □
Follow Route 254 on the left-hand side of the Canton Valley, heading right downhill over green slopes. Go right to cross the Rio Colorin and then head southeast (Route 255) through a splendid mountain forest. On coming to the broad pasturelands of Pian dei Mughi, take the nearby track to the Malga Ritorto, from where there are more good views. An unsurfaced road carries us from here northwards along wooded slopes; we pass below the cabin lift and come to the settlement of Patascoss, on a wide pause in the mountain. Here we turn right to follow the red-paint waymarking east downhill to Madonna di Campiglio.

Opposite: the Brenta Group from Lake Ritorto

INDEX

Numbers following entries are *walk* numbers, *not* page numbers. For mountain groups, see Contents. Spellings below (whether German or Italian) correspond to those used for the *walk title and the walking maps*; in the text itself, many terms have been translated into English.